Ex arte adj. [eks är´-tā];
derivation of the Latin
expression 'according to the
principles of art'...............
............'beauty through art'...

—Glossary of Latin Words

Published by

P A N A C H E   P A R T N E R S

Panache Partners, LLC
1424 Gables Court
Plano, Texas 75075
469.246.6060
Fax: 469.246.6062
www.panache.com

Publishers: Brian G. Carabet and John A. Shand

Printed in China

Distributed by Independent Publishers Group
800.888.4741

PUBLISHER'S DATA

Geoffrey Bradfield: Ex Arte

Library of Congress Control Number: 2008943792
ISBN 13: 978-1-933415-78-9
ISBN 10: 1-933415-78-9

For information about custom editions, special
sales, premium and corporate books, please
contact Panache Partners at
bcarabet@panache.com

First Printing 2009
10 9 8 7 6 5 4 3 2 1

Panache Partners, LLC and Geoffrey Bradfield Inc.
are dedicated to the restoration and conservation
of the environment.

Our books are manufactured with strict adherence
to an environmental management system in
accordance with ISO 14001 standards, including
the use of paper from mills certified to derive their
products from environmentally managed forests.
We are committed to continued investigation of
alternative paper products and environmentally
responsible manufacturing processes to ensure
the preservation of our fragile planet.

PHOTO CREDITS
By Simon Alexander: 13; 28; 359.
By Robert Brantley: 5; 186-201; 252-275.
By Ruth Cincotta: 234-237.
By Sean Finnigan: 276-293.
By Scott Frances, Courtesy *Architectural Digest*, © 2006.
The Conde Nast Publication. Used with permission: 52;
54-56; 58; 61-62; 64; 67-68; 70; 73.
By Gianni Franchellucci: 46.
By John Lei: 352-358.
By Cutty McGill: 24-26.
By Jaideep Oberoi: 310-319.
By Peter Rymwid: 152-167; 320-337; 340-341; 344-351.
By Kim Sargent: 204-231; 238-251.
By H. Durston Saylor: End Papers; 29-45; 47-48; 75-139;
168-179.
By H. Durston Saylor, Courtesy *Architectural Digest*,
© 2005. *The Conde Nast Publication*. Used with
permission: 49; 51.
By H. Durston Saylor, Courtesy *Architectural Digest*,
© 2004. *The Conde Nast Publication*. Used with
permission: 140; 142; 144; 146; 148; 150.
By H. Durston Saylor, Courtesy *Architectural Digest*,
© 2008. *The Conde Nast Publication*. Used with
permission: Front Cover; 295; 296; 298; 301; 303; 304;
306; 309; Back Cover.

Renderings by Alberto Cordoneda: 106; 180; 183; 184;
190; 326; 341; 342.

GEOFFREY BRADFIELD
EX ARTE

with Jorge S. Arango

Principal Photographer Durston Saylor

TABLE OF CONTENTS

ACKNOWLEDGMENTS

I cannot begin to thank anyone without first acknowledging the enormous debt of gratitude due Paige Rense, Editor-in-Chief of *Architectural Digest*. Not only for her foreword to this book, but also for generously granting permission to use photography from the *Condé Nast* archives that was crucial to this book. Her recognition of my work and her support over the years have been incalculable.

I wish to give special thanks to my associate, Roric Tobin, whose contribution to this project has been invaluable to me. I must also acknowledge the creative efforts of my in-house graphic designer Justyna Watorek. And, not least, Helena Lehane and Ayesha Khan for their keen critique and encouragement.

Thanks to the staff at Panache, especially co-founder Brian Carabet, regional publisher Paul Geiger, senior designer Emily Kattan and editor Rosalie Wilson for their support and patience—much needed virtues when working alongside a typical Virgo.

We are only as good as our clients allow us to be. This book could never have been realized without the cooperation of these wonderful patrons, who had the courage earlier on to respond to my creative challenge. To them I extend my warmest thanks. It was, quite literally, where it all began.

It takes a unique eye to capture the spirit of my work. Thanks to all the exceptional photographers with whom I've had the privilege of working on this project, among them Durston Saylor, Sean Finnigan, Robert Brantley, Kim Sargent, Peter Rymwid, Scott Frances, Simon Alexander, Ruth Cincotta, Gianni Franchellucci and Jaideep Oberoi.

Also indispensable to the production of this book was my writer, Jorge Arango, someone I can honestly say "gets me." By synthesizing dense biographical information and historical references with his own knowledge of art and design, he has succeeded in capturing my inner voice.

Lastly, many people offer kind assessments of my character and my work throughout this book. To those artists, gallery owners, collectors, antiques dealers and dear friends I extend my heartfelt thanks. "A man is known by the company he keeps," goes the old saying, and it has been my honour to have shared this mortal plane with their gracious company.

—Geoffrey Bradfield

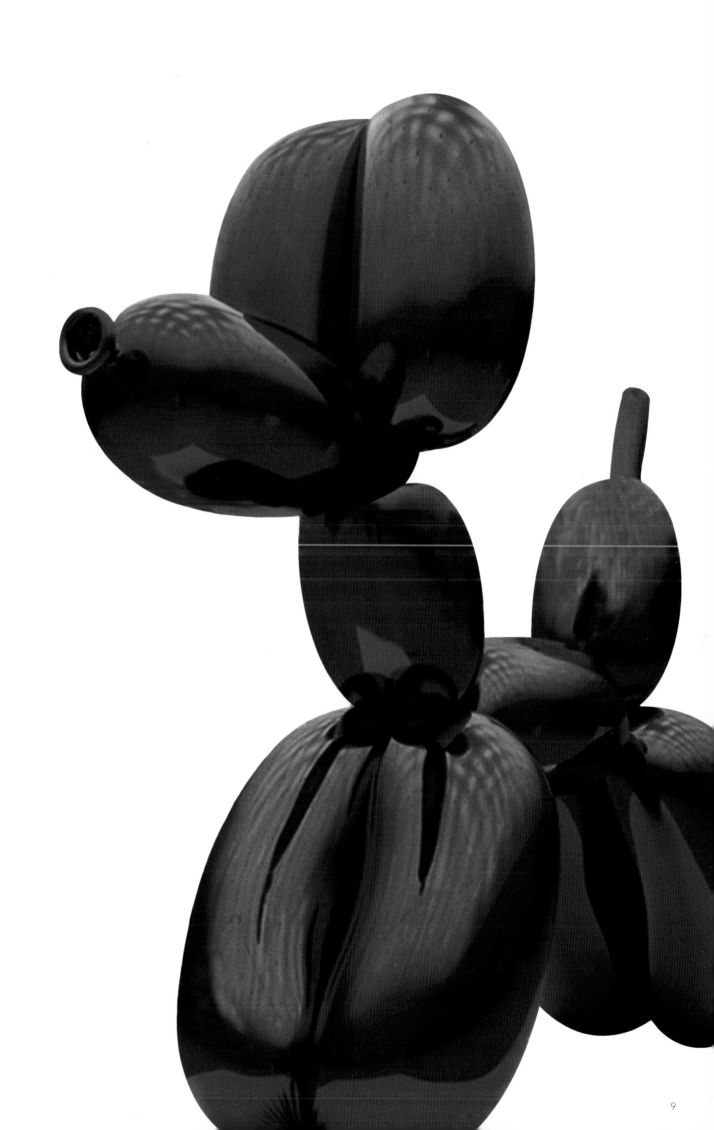

FOREWORD

Every good story has a beginning, middle and an end. Geoffrey Bradfield's story begins in South Africa where he lived a rather privileged life and enjoyed a classic education, which likely formed the foundation for his Neo-classic point of view.

The middle of his story begins in New York City, where he quickly found a place in the studios of a handful of well-established designers, leading to his fortuitous meeting and subsequent professional partnership with the late, legendary Jay Spectre. At the time, Jay was about as famous as an interior designer could be. *Architectural Digest* had shown his work many times throughout several decades. For Jay to choose Geoffrey Bradfield as a partner was more than a vote of confidence; it was the equivalent of being knighted. They worked very successfully together for the rest of Jay's too-short life.

We are further along now, approaching the point of climax in the arc of Geoffrey's exceptional tale. I admit that, at first, I simply didn't know whether Geoffrey had the enormous talent it would take to live up to Jay's reputation. But I was fond of Geoffrey and hoped for the best. That's what I got…and more. With each new commission, Geoffrey Bradfield's design viewpoint became stronger and stronger and more unique to his extraordinary talent.

That talent created quite a stir in the design world, a stir to which I was happy to add momentum by publishing his work again and again in *Architectural Digest* over the years. I also like to think that our confidence and support helped bring about a major plot development in Geoffrey's story too. Stark brought his look to their showrooms with the Geoffrey Bradfield Collection of furniture, carpets, wallpaper and fabrics—a grand slam with the Neo-classic designs so on-target for today. His work with heavy acrylic that is molded into traditional furniture forms was spot-on for the many who had tired of heavy brownness and endless beige.

Geoffrey's work is inspired and original. Its historical references are clear, yet the contemporary vocabulary renders it absolutely unique. He has accomplished a design tour de force. As this book makes clear, the end is not here and not near. Geoffrey Bradfield's story will never end.

—Paige Rense
Editor-in-Chief of *Architectural Digest*

INTRODUCTION

"Great artists have always influenced and inspired my work. I admire their ability to look at the world from fresh and daring perspectives. An unconventional way of synthesizing their genius in both word and art challenges the soul and opens the door to entire universes of new thought. At times the simplicity of this vision has a profound elemental grace and beauty. The truest of these is a summation I am wont to share with Constantin Brancusi: 'Don't look for obscure formulas or mystery in my work...It is pure joy that I offer you.'"

—Geoffrey Bradfield

Geoffrey Bradfield's rooms truly are like Piet Mondrian's exquisitely calibrated paintings. Move a single block of color in that artist's irregular grids and the harmony of the composition falls completely apart. Similarly, Bradfield's designs are so clearly conceived and executed that there really is no other way to think of them. One would be hard-pressed to find an alternative spot for those priceless Jacob divans, or better suited fixtures for a particular wall than the Ruhlmann sconces, or a more appropriate setting for the monumental Frankenthaler painting, or the Nevelson, Schnabel, Marden, Newman or Lichtenstein...

The designer's A-list clients return to him repeatedly for each new project, entrusting him to deliver a perfectly crystallized, consummately luxurious vision. In the eloquent words of one longtime client: "He is, in his field, like Frank Lloyd Wright was in architecture, or Picasso in painting, or Thoreau in literature. His work is transcendental. He takes you into his world and you are engulfed by a different sensibility. It changes the way you see. I think of Geoffrey as a great artist."

To equate Bradfield with fine artists is not mere grandiloquence. His work employs the same tools, aptitudes and concepts artists utilize in the creation of their own masterpieces: color, texture, form, composition, intellect, art reference and historical allusion. Since the very beginning of his career he has championed the oeuvre of a vast coterie of painters and sculptors, many of them emerging at the time he began acquiring their works for clients. Indeed, the audacious use of bold contemporary art in his interiors is widely recognized as one of Bradfield's signatures. He is an inveterate collector of quotations by artists that explain their view of the world. Many of them head the chapters of this book.

And the designer has an artist's intrepid spirit, determined as he is to follow his own vision without regard to popular fashion. "One must keep in mind that interior design is not an exact science," says Bradfield, echoing Robert Rauschenberg's belief that "anything you do will be an abuse of somebody else's aesthetics," an assertion he stands by with fearless confidence.

"My passion for art, and my fascination with those who create it," he says, "has led me to meet many extraordinary talents." Among the privileged encounters Bradfield has had over the years, he can count Diego Giacometti, Andy Warhol, Jean-Michel Basquiat, Fernando Botero, Jeff Koons, Tom Wesselman and Kenneth Noland. "It's all about my ongoing search for the visually sublime."

Jean-Gabriel Mitterand, the Parisian art dealer with whom Bradfield has worked for years to acquire the art of Claude and François-Xavier Lalanne, says, "Together we share a love of Lalanne sculpture. Geoffrey recognizes that the Lalannes are the last living artists of another world, that of sophistication, and one belonging to the recent past—Marie-Helene de Rothschild, Natalie de Noialles, Yves Saint Laurent—and that their fantastical impression on our imagination is made of surrealistic invention and charm. Sometimes art is too strong for the architect's ego. But not for Geoffrey Bradfield, who has always loved to mix art and style. It is extremely rare to find a professional like Geoffrey, who dedicates his life to high-end architecture, with a refined sense of decoration, and at the same time cultivates a passion for art."

Born in 1946, Bradfield was raised on a farm in South Africa, a country, he says, that "was part of the waning British Empire. It was a time warp, a civilization that has long since vanished." Athlone, the family home bordering the Transkei in the Eastern Cape, "had no architectural merit to speak of," he recalls. "It was solid and unadorned, and resembled something rather like a fortress. But what it lacked in artistic merit it made up for in scale." Built on a promontory with commanding views of the Indian Ocean, it was Bradfield's first exposure to grandly proportioned rooms. Their imprint would forever inform his sense of graciousness and scale. The fastidious English manners and decorum that permeated his childhood have stayed with him throughout his life.

While still a teenager, Bradfield circumnavigated the globe, a journey that not only rounded out his already polished education, but also bred astute social skills and a sharp wit that would gain him introduction to an enormous array of the creative personages of the time. He began in London in the mid 1960s, alighting there during the glam rock heyday of Carnaby Street and Kings Road, of Hockney, Quant and Sassoon. There he cultivated an appreciation for the high life. "As a teenager I was befriended by the late Venetian, Baron Alessandro Albrizzi and his partner Tony Cloughley," he says fondly, "Their lifestyle was amazing, elegant yet unpretentious, and their furniture designs at the time were a marked inspiration." He also grew to know Anthony Redmile, the eccentric 1960s-70s designer who sold, from his Kings Road shop, inventive tortoiseshell, antler and shell furniture that was "far out" and all the rage.

Bradfield made his way to Canada at the pinnacle of the flower child culture, then traversed the United States, pausing in San Francisco to absorb the groundbreaking energy of Haight-Ashbury, before setting sail for the Pacific Rim. When anchored in Hong Kong's Victoria Harbor, he was chauffered off to a guided tour of the Peninsula Hotel. "We entered the world-famous Marco Polo Suite—announced," goes one typical diary entry. "So many people everywhere and…none other than Noël Coward, breakfasting, no less…he touched my hand politely, barely taking me in—so grand." On board that same ship he met a lecherous Ramon Navarro, the once handsome silent screen heartthrob of classics like *Ben-Hur* and *Mata Hari.* "He reminds me of the frog prince," wrote Bradfield. "At least he looks like a frog—sad, watery eyes. How cruel age."

Upon his return to South Africa, Bradfield and two partners established their own design firm. Based in Johannesburg, the company was instantly successful, executing substantial projects in Tel Aviv, America, London and other international locales and receiving, among a slew of unusual commissions, the furnishing of the royal kraal and throne room for King Sobhuza II of Swaziland. "His majesty had a preference for contemporary, so I imported from Switzerland 24 de Sede chairs in steel and scarlet leather. We had the leather monogrammed with a coronet at the king's request. The contrast was startling and I don't think the royal kraal ever quite recovered."

It was through his Johannesburg company that he met the late David Hicks and many other noted designers of the day. He also shared an amusing friendship with Erté in Paris, having crossed paths with him at the Alcazar. This diminutive Art Deco illustrator introduced Bradfield to the louche underbelly of the city. On trips to Milan for the furniture fairs, he made the acquaintance of the renowned architect Gae Aulenti and über-talented Willy Rizzo (then married to the stunning actress Elsa Martinelli). Another friendship was forged with art dealer Luciano Anselmino, who represented Andy Warhol in Europe. Staying in Anselmino's home during one of these trips, he encountered Warhol for the first time, in Milan for a press conference. The reporters "were desperate, getting nothing but monosyllables" from the artist, Bradfield recalls. "Then a very pretty reporter asked him whether there was any continuity between a painting he did on one day and one he did on the next. Suddenly he came to life and uttered an emphatic, 'No!' The atmosphere was electric. After an interminable pause, he added, 'Because I dream at night.' It was brilliant. The next day that was the headline in all the international papers."

Bradfield left South Africa in 1977 to fulfill his dream of living in Manhattan, an island that had beguiled him from a very early age. He accepted a position with the venerable decorating firm McMillen Inc. and worked for the legendary Eleanor Brown and indomitable Betty Sherrill, thence becoming partner with Jay Spectre. He remained with Spectre for 14 fruitful and prolific years, until the designer's untimely death in 1992, when Bradfield reorganized the company under his own name.

Bradfield and Spectre's high-end clientele expanded his social circle exponentially. In the 1970s, while working for the daughter of Jack Warner, Barbara Howard, and her producer husband Cy, Bradfield was introduced to Cecil Beaton, "the vainest man I ever met. I enjoyed a surreal evening transfixed by his minute duplex flat in the Sherry-Netherland, almost entirely composed of an astonishing staircase adorned with enamel suits of playing cards. Sheer wizardry, and typical Beaton stagecraft." As a frequent guest at Clarence House founder Robin Roberts's country estate, Bradfield would find himself sitting at any given time beside the likes of actress Candice Bergen, the Broadway producer Dasha Epstein, Senator Patrick Moynihan and fashion designer Pauline Trigère. Princess Elizabeth of Yugoslavia was a constant companion at New York's many glittering galas. "We would end up at all the Harlem clubs together in the small hours of the morning—Jimmy's Uptown, Brown Sugar and Jimmy's Bronx Café. I'd be in white tie and tails and she would be in a ball gown, no one batting an eye."

It was during these two giddy, charmed decades that Bradfield began establishing lasting relationships with a roster of major artistic talents. He and Spectre visited Diego Giacometti's studio in Paris on many occasions, commissioning specific pieces from his atelier. Louise Nevelson created installations on several of their projects. "She was such an original—all that kohl and drama," says Bradfield. "It was borderline kabuki, but there was a discipline to her look. She knew exactly who she was." He has breakfasted with the Lalannes in their walled fantasy garden outside Paris, dined with David Hockney and with Jeff Koons. Visiting Miguel Ortiz Berrocal's elaborate palazzo in Verona, with its lush formal grounds and mind-teasing puzzle sculptures, Bradfield found himself surrounded by a clowder of the artist's domesticated ocelots. "Each of these visits a visual feast, artists living in their own fascinating realm of originality and imagination."

There were famous art patrons as well, among them his revered friend Henry McIlhenny, "the last Edwardian," as Bradfield describes him. "His Impressionist collection was unrivalled and, although he lived on a grand scale—a magnificent castle in Ireland and the most important residence on Rittenhouse Square—it never felt like visiting a museum." Bradfield also recounts working on a townhouse for Frederick Weisman in the late 1970s. On an occasion, to meet a social deadline, the renowned entrepreneur and collector had insisted that a recent purchase of a Noguchi honed granite coffee table be hoisted by crane to the sixth-floor lounge. Bradfield worked tirelessly all day to achieve this complicated maneuver and ready the place for cocktails, which would be followed by yet another night at Studio 54. Guests began to arrive, among them Warhol, who by then was an ubiquitous habitué of the party circuit. "When the feat was completed, I mixed myself a well-deserved drink and sank into a sofa," says Bradfield. "To my horror, I looked down to witness a black line racing toward me at some speed, like a snake slithering across the marble surface. The staggering weight of the granite table had sent a serious crack through the floor! We had to vacate the building post haste."

Bradfield's social forays are filled with such stories. One night Spectre and he took a table at a gala for the Metropolitan Museum's Costume Institute. Ethel Scull, the first patron to commission a portrait from Warhol, was invited. "The Bentley was sent round to collect her four times," says Bradfield. "She never arrived." Later on, everyone reconvened at the 21 Club where, finally, Scull made her appearance. "Jay asked her if she wanted something to eat, and she said, 'I'll just have a snack.' She proceeded to order $2,000 or $3,000 worth of caviar and made this massive sandwich with it. As she prepared to put it to her mouth she said, 'Isn't life a sandwich of sh--?' She was a nightmare. Her every action was studied 'Pop Art.' Poor lass died penniless."

All of these artists and collectors continue to influence and enrich Bradfield's work today. He has been called, not surprisingly, "the Billionaire's Designer." His discerning eye and his knowledge of art and decoration, his natural modesty and charm in prominent circles such as these, as well as his exacting level of professionalism, garnered Bradfield, in 2005, a coveted title of "Dean of American Design" from *Architectural Digest*. The venerable publication has perennially included him on its prestigious AD 100 list. Television shows continue and include a profile on CNBC's "High Net Worth" as well as a one-hour special on the workings of his company on HGTV. He continues to be featured internationally in countless magazines and influential publications. The firm enjoys such global renown that it has expanded its reach to include companies in Dubai and Qatar.

In late 2008 he earned a place on *Haute Living*'s Haute 100 list, which identifies the most influential people in the world living in New York. "As the designer of choice for billionaires everywhere," said the editors, "Bradfield's impeccable taste can be seen in some of the city's most spectacular residences." The designer was especially honored to receive a tribute bestowed upon him by his mother country. Archbishop Desmond M. Tutu presented him in 2007 with the Phelophepa Train Award (the miracle train is a mobile medical unit that travels to South African rural areas providing health-related services to the poor). "Our gratitude to Geoffrey Bradfield for his love, compassion and continued support to his homeland…," said Archbishop Tutu at the ceremonies. "I have the immense pleasure of greeting him as our guest of honor at this very special event in recognition of his sterling success globally as one of the most inspiring and internationally acclaimed designers of our time."

In 2004 Bradfield published the critically acclaimed volume *Defining Millennium Modern*, a book called a "must read" by the organizers of Art Basel Miami, who cited it as a textbook for using modern and contemporary art in interiors. French cultural critic Antoine du Rocher assured readers that it deftly illustrated how best to "integrate a significant modern or contemporary work of art into a private residence without it overwhelming an interior or simply looking like a work for sale in a Manhattan gallery or on view in a museum."

Ex Arte, Bradfield's follow-up to *Millennium Modern*, focuses on this last, and perhaps most ardent, of his passions. It should serve as a testament to his place as one of the world's most fervent advocates of the art of our times. While Bradfield is cognizant of fashionable collecting, investment value and creating a design legacy, it must be said that his impulses and vision spring more simply from an innate elixir, not unlike Brancusi's: "It is pure joy that I offer you."

"…to him, life itself was the first, the greatest of the arts…all the others seemed to be but a preparation."

—Oscar Wilde, from *The Picture of Dorian Gray*

In a remembrance that appeared in London's *Daily Telegraph* shortly after his death, the Baron de Rédé was described as living "a self-imposed life of exquisite perfection," the tongue-in-cheek implication being, of course, that it had been an arduous endurance for the poor man. If so, pity Geoffrey Bradfield, for he has thrust upon himself similarly demanding parameters. Based on decades of ever-mounting evidence and a life replete with fabulous parties, it is safe to say he is a person who relishes the same exquisite hardship.

If the designer's rooms are as precisely calibrated as Piet Mondrian's paintings, then his social whirl is like Mondrian's famous "Broadway Boogie Woogie": restless, pulsing, colorful, vibrant, joyous, refined and filled with rhythm and life. His parties are invariably indelible. "I've always entertained, no matter how modest my homes have been," says Bradfield. "My parents were socially inclusive and the most generous hosts, never pretentious. There was always room at my parents' table for one more guest."

Their generosity has carried through. Over the years Bradfield has fêted New York and Palm Beach's beau monde with ever more elaborate gatherings. "Geoffrey gives from the heart," says fashion designer Eric Javits. "He wants everyone to open themselves up and experience life through his eyes. That's why he loves entertaining; he revels in the exchange. He's always eager to share his stories and hear everyone else's."

For couturier Douglas Hannant, Bradfield once hosted a Persian dinner that required the tailoring of lavish costumes imported from Thailand and the removal of French doors from the reception room of White Hall in order to accommodate the 82 guests at a single long table. The table, which Hannant remembers was decorated with antique carved dragons, "extended from Geoffrey's sleek white marble foyer into the garden, which was tented in pleated chartreuse fabric. It was certainly an evening never to be forgotten!" For his associate Roric Tobin's 30th birthday, he dreamt up an "Opium" party. "No gifts, please," read the invitation, "just your indulgence. Asian attire or black tie." Nearly 300 guests showed up in kimonos, saris and Fu Manchu moustaches, dining amidst several million dollars worth of loaned Chinese antiquities.

Lavishly themed parties today are a rarity (or worse, just plain dull). But Bradfield stylishly honors this tradition, which has a long and distinguished lineage: it stretches at least as far back as the Roman bacchanalias, continues through Renaissance commedia dell'arte balls and Ludwig II's grotto entertainments, on to Rédé's Bal de têtes and Bal Orientale, Capote's mythic Black and

PREVIOUS PAGES: Bradfield, captured in a film still, on a mine dump on the outskirts of Johannesburg in his early 20s.

THESE PAGES: A Bradfield timeline, from infancy to today.

White party and Malcolm Forbes's Moorish fantasia in Morocco. From his early teens, Bradfield was a natural-born host. His sense of old-world elegance was already considerably evolved at 16, when he threw a party with a formal dress code. "How many 16-year-olds would get all of their friends into black tie and ball gowns?" he sighs. "I loved doing it and ever since have never had a generic party." (A "Farewell to Arms" party upon the completion of his South African military service and a bon voyage party when he left Africa for Europe, where he enlisted his younger brother, a renowned engineer-in-the-making, to orchestrate an elaborate fireworks display, are just two early examples.)

Bradfield is a quintessentially social being, which means he is as coveted a guest as he is a celebrated host. Dinners at Windsor Castle and Buckingham Palace are not unusual invitations for him. Possessed of an indefatigable energy honed during the salad days of the disco era, his thirst for the good life is insatiable. He knows what it is to be a night owl. The Oscar-winning actress Claire Trevor knew she could ring him at all hours. "She used to live next door to me on Fifth Avenue," recalls Bradfield fondly. "She would wait until my lights went on after I returned from the clubs and call. 'Darling,' she would say, 'Come over and watch a movie with me'…Try telling a Hollywood star that it's two o'clock in the morning and one has to work the next day. Ever persuasive, vodka on the rocks with a slice of orange was Claire's poison. We'd share a sandwich from the Pierre's restaurant downstairs and watch not one, but two, movies! Believe it or not, I'd be petal-fresh the next morning."

Through Trevor and others he met scores of celebrities, including Jane Powell ("compassionate animal lover"), Bette Davis ("cranky"), Van Johnson ("a charmer"), Rock ("call me Roy") Hudson. Gypsy Rose Lee's sister Baby June, Kitty Carlisle Hart ("vivacious"), Marisa Berenson ("a true aristocrat"), Claudette Colbert ("forever young") and the writer, director and producer Joe Mankiewicz (*Philadelphia Story, All About Eve, Cleopatra*). "He was an extraordinary man," remembers Bradfield. "Aided by a trach tube, Joe would always say, 'Come sit beside me; I know you want to talk about Bette'—and indeed I could never get enough of his Tinseltown stories."

Over the years, Bradfield has hosted every manner of celebration: a Midas Touch dinner here, a Native American reception there. "Geoffrey Bradfield is the only man in New York these days who gives a private cocktail and sit-down dinner for 20, 40 or 60 people," says David Patrick Columbia, founder of the *New York Social Diary* and a diarist à la Samuel Pepys of our age. "He entertains the same way he designs and decorates the homes of his clients, with them in mind, and it's always impeccable."

BRADFIELD BOO

GIE WOOGIE

The Ball at Milbank House

The venue for Geoffrey Bradfield's 60th Birthday was the palatial 26-room Upper East Side mansion, formerly owned by the Milbank family—a setting truly befitting a dean of design. The theme for the lavish soirée was hinted at in the stiff white invitations that read, "Please no gifts, rather ball gowns in black or silver and diamonds." Bradfield's liveried footmen were dressed in black and gold brocade frock coats, white stockings and knee breeches with buckled shoes and powdered wigs—all custom designed by Bradfield. Live models were painted as blackamoors, decorated with Swarovski crystals and ostrich plumes. They posed as sentinels, guarding the front door and flanking the entrance to the grand ballroom where Alex Donner's orchestra played everything from Cole Porter to more contemporary favorites, while guests danced and feasted on an endless supper. The 400-guest list read like a who's who roll call of New York. In attendance were international diplomats, dignitaries and socialites. Breakfast was served at 1 a.m. and the festivities carried on well into the morning hours.

PREVIOUS TWO PAGES: The designer and friends…many, many friends.

THESE PAGES: The host entertaining guests at White Hall during a pre-ball supper for 24 guests, attended by footmen in Bradfield-designed livery.

FOLLOWING PAGE TOP: A peacock wearing a 60-carat diamond necklace (top) is the newel ornament on a white marble staircase lined with footmen in 18th-century costumes.

FOLLOWING PAGE BOTTOM: Bradfield and his attendants in the subterranean Neoclassical pool of the Milbank house.

It is impossible to separate the man from the lifestyle. The socially acute fashion icon Iris Apfel observes: "Geoffrey Bradfield is my fantasy of that perfect Edwardian gentleman: exquisitely mannered, impeccably tailored, well spoken, conversationally witty, politically savvy. His great fund of knowledge is combined with tremendous generosity of spirit. Then there is the exquisite taste with which he plies his craft. This places him professionally as one of our leading interior designers, much sought after by clients, much praised by the press as well as his peers. And then there is his private passion for parties. He gives some of the very best ever. Since I had the good fortune of meeting him several years ago, I've had the extreme pleasure of attending three genuine blockbusters. From the eclectic cast of invitees to the yummy food, the offbeat venues and the dashing outfits, to the over-the-top décor, they rate a highly charged WOW! Carl and I feel very honored to be included on his guest list."

The designer Carleton Varney speaks with equal fondness and admiration. Bradfield's talents as a host, Varney says, start with his sense of style and the clarity of his vision. "There are very few people in this business whom I feel have a sense of 'It,'" he says. "Dorothy Draper created a look, Frank Lloyd Wright created a look, Michael Taylor and John Saladino created a look. Geoffrey doesn't just do a room; he creates a look. And that is his major talent. Most people in this industry today grew up not knowing one thing: glamour. They want to touch it, but they don't know it. Geoffrey knows glamour, he lives glamour."

Bradfield spends an inordinate amount of time on planning his parties, and it shows, says Eric Javits. "A sense of theater underlies Geoffrey's parties. He's a design visionary, which also extends to his entertaining. Geoffrey's creative mind works everything out."

Varney adds, "Every detail—from the hors d'oeuvres to the tablecloth to the invitations to the flowers—he doesn't miss a trick, he really thinks about it. That's art."

When Bradfield begins reminiscing about his years of party-going and party-throwing, he does mention the one invitation that he most cherishes: One from the late Queen Mother to design a dinner for 100 guests at St. James's Palace. A devout Anglican, Bradfield and the Queen Mother were active in the Sloane Square Church charity in London, and just months before she passed away she approached him to create the table settings for this cause, which was dear to her heart. "It was the most wonderful honor," he says.

It was an honor well deserved, another moment in "a life of exquisite perfection."

ABOVE: For the dinner at St. James's Palace commissioned by Her Majesty, the Queen Mother, Bradfield designed over-scaled floral table centerpieces—inspired by her coronation crown—using white carnations, purple statice, white tuberose and silver-sprayed vines.

"A man's life is his image."

—*Velvet Goldmine*

As the American poet Richard Eberhart once said, "Style is the perfection of a point of view." One can trace this process in the life of any artist—whether painter, writer, dancer or musician—and witness the moment in which that point of view blossoms into an identifiable style.

It is no different with designers, whose private residences, of course, are laboratories for the evolution of their taste. "Designing for oneself is completely selfish and indulgent," says Bradfield. "With no client looking over your shoulder you can really express yourself and push the envelope." One must assume, then, that Bradfield's own home embodies his most adventurous ideas and resolves them into a cohesive whole that we recognize as Bradfield style.

That style is as fastidious as his personal appearance. This becomes immediately apparent as soon as guests are ushered through the threshold of White Hall, his über-elegant townhouse on Park Avenue and 61st Street in Manhattan. Bradfield epitomizes decorum and dash. Always the best-dressed man in the room, he favors starched collars, perfectly tailored pinstripe suits (though in summer you can find him head-to-toe in pink seersucker) and a carriage at once formal and wry—Cary Grant, say, crossed with Sir John Gielgud.

This fastidiousness translates into rigorously edited interiors at White Hall. There is not a single extraneous element in this environment; all of it is as considered as his meticulously knotted ties. White limestone floors stretch down a hall from the front door, past a photomural of his street that was enlarged from a 1930s black-and-white photograph, to a reception room with French doors leading into a courtyard garden. The inspiration for this room, he explains, came from a visit to Helena Rubenstein's apartment at Quai Bethune on the Île Saint-Louis in Paris. "It has always haunted me," says Bradfield, "the pure symmetry and Palladian order of that room, with plain columns and Ionic capitals."

The room borrows ideas from the Rubenstein flat, but deploys them with a chic spareness that heightens the sense of refinement. Twelve white columns—with Ionic capitals, of course—file neatly down each side of the reception room and continue outside into the courtyard, giving the impression of an endlessly long gallery. Mirrored walls between the columns inside, and an arched mirror at the end of the courtyard, amplify the feeling of infinite space, a room without walls. Were it not for the urban setting and the reductive modernism, you could think you were in Palladio's Villa Foscari.

Rubenstein deployed acrylic furniture in her famous Paris apartment, and here Bradfield does the same with "Lady Mendl" klismos chairs and a Neoclassical "Medici" table from his furniture collection. Their ghost-like silhouettes ensure that the long view remains intact. The room is perfection, Palladio interpreted through a modern prism. Yet its formalism also accommodates Bradfield's wry wit. Jean Cocteau's surrealist "Beast" sconces protrude from the mirrored walls, seemingly proffering draped torches to guests before they venture outside. And 19th-century French bérgères have dove-gray upholstery on the front, but if one looks in the mirrored wall, they reveal a racy Schiaparelli pink Ultrasuede on their backs. The room can host an intimate dinner or, when Bradfield feels like really throwing a party, a table seating a hundred can extend from inside, through the French doors clear into the courtyard.

The drawing room is perhaps Bradfield's most audacious statement. "Everything here is about surprise," he explains. "The room reflects my infatuation with the 1940s—the decade of my birth. But, I was not trying to re-create a period room. I wanted to capture our moment in time. If someone were to look back at this room in the future, they would absolutely know it was designed at the turn of this millennium."

OPENING PAGES: Bradfield's townhouse (left), originally built in 1869. The entrance hall (right) leads to the reception room past a blown up vintage photograph of the townhouse from the 1930s and Sabin Howard's "Hermes" sculpture.

SECOND SPREAD: The symmetry and Palladian order of the reception room were inspired by a visit to Helena Rubenstein's apartment on the Île Saint-Louis in Paris. Bradfield's acrylic "Medici" table and "Lady Mendl" chairs are the central axis of the room. Nineteenth-century bérgères sport dove gray Ultrasuede in front and Schiaparelli pink Ultrasuede behind.

PREVIOUS PAGES: Julian Schnabel's "Elvira" oil on velvet is the focus on the wall opposite the fireplace. The French table at right supports a ceramic Fornasetti Roman foot sculpture.

LEFT: The custom fireplace with paladium side ornamentation and Gilbert Poillerat andirons in white gold.

FOLLOWING PAGES: The classical fieldstone courtyard beyond the reception room was kept deliberately spare to accommodate large gatherings. Its boldest gestures are an arch-framed mirror that gives the impression of an additional garden beyond and Joel Perlman's "Straight Up" steel sculpture.

To those future observers, it would be obvious that the millennium ended on a rather glamorous note. The room's palette spans the subtle colorations of an oyster shell—from silver and gray-blue to pearly white. A deeply cut-pile rug swirls with graceful, Gilbert Poillerat-inspired gray foliage underfoot. An extravagance of silk taffeta curtains, quilted Chanel-like at the bottoms, drapes luxuriously from the Neoclassical moldings. "Designed to puddle heavily on the floor," says Bradfield, "they're reminiscent of ball gowns—and very voluptuous." Two 19th-century French side tables, finished in matte white with silver ormolu trappings, bracket Bradfield's "DD" (as in Dorothy Duke) sofa. His acrylic wingback chairs and "Clear Conscience" low table add Hollywood flair. Custom Ruhlmann-inspired chrome sconces shed light that is amplified by huge panel mirrors set into the dove white-colored boiserie.

The art brings a contemporary sophistication to the surroundings: Julian Schnabel's "Carey" behind the sofa, Jeff Koons's porcelain "Puppy" on a side table, Sophia Vari's marble "Centaure" sculpture on the low table, and François-Xavier Lalanne's patinated bronze "Oiseau Bleu II" on a white bombé chest. Above the modern fireplace, which is sleekly low and long, Rachel Hovnanian's "Narcissus, White on White II" explores a painterly and meditative depth of space.

The library-cum-media room exists almost completely within the spectrum of the silver screen. Bradfield extended the room 12 feet, creating a raised seating area defined by a tufted and fringed, U-shaped pale gray built-in sofa. A crown molding with platinum disks encircles the room. The exceptions to the monochromatic scheme are accents of brilliant blue that derive from an Yves Klein coffee table of acrylic filled with vivid cobalt-blue pigment.

PREVIOUS PAGES: "Everything here is about surprise," says Bradfield of the drawing room. "This room reflects my infatuation with the 1940s—the decade of my birth." But the designer updates the Art Moderne look with a restrained elegance, silvery-gray color scheme and modern art, which includes a Jeff Koons "Puppy" on the side table.

RIGHT: A custom-designed carpet and "DD" sofa, acrylic "Signature Wingback" chairs and a "Clear Conscience" coffee table from Bradfield's Millennium Modern collection form the main seating area of the drawing room below Julian Schnabel's "Carey," an oil on velvet. Sophia Vari's white marble "Centaure" sculpture is on the coffee table.

"I love Geoffrey's interiors because he recognizes that the home is a refuge. He understands the need for tranquility in day-to-day life, and he is able to create an environment that's an artistic sanctuary."

—Rachel Hovnanian

LEFT: Keeping the fireplace low and long emphasizes the verticality of the drawing room (left). Rachel Hovnanian's "Narcissus, White on White II" hangs above. Karel Nel's oval painting "Ancestral Void" and Joel Perlman's nickel-bronze "Perfect Storm II" are reflected in the mirrored panel to the right of the fireplace. On the left is a bombé chest atop which sits François-Xavier Lalanne's patinated bronze "Oiseau Bleu II."

ABOVE: Artist Rachel Hovnanian in her studio working on "Narcissus, White on White II." Bradfield was instantly attracted to Hovnanian's work because, he says, it "explores meditation and inner peace."

"Art is central to our species
and our society."

—*Robert Redford*

PREVIOUS PAGES: Bradfield extended his library 12 feet, cantilevering it over the reception room. The centerpiece here is an Yves Klein blue pigment coffee table from Sotheby's, which sets the accent color for the rest of the room.

ABOVE: Artglass spheres on the Klein table with custom-designed andirons in the background.

RIGHT: Above a custom settee, a Louise Nevelson wood construction levitates in the middle of a mirrored wall. Fletcher Benton's painted steel "Folded Square Alphabet R" is in the foreground.

"In the master bedroom, Bradfield channeled the debonair Billy Haines. The room telegraphs a well-dressed serenity…and showcases discreetly stunning modern art."

LEFT: The playful Bradfield-designed rug hints at the nonchalance of a room that Bradfield wanted "to be undecorated and have a loose approach to furnishings." Milton Avery's "Pink Dunes" sits on an easel from Bradfield's Millennium Modern collection. Over the fireplace, fronted by two "Coco" chairs from the collection, is Julie Hedrick's "White Dawn."

ABOVE: Kenneth Noland's nine-foot-long "Untitled" from 1971 floats above a bed with a custom-designed headboard and a Dennis Basso chinchilla throw. Niki de Saint-Phalle's "Magic Bird" is on the bedside table.

> *"I believe that if one's work has resonance, it will outlive us."*
>
> —*Geoffrey Bradfield*

In the master bedroom, Bradfield channeled the debonair Billy Haines. The room telegraphs a well-dressed serenity. Low-slung furnishings instantly draw one's energy calmly downward. Tufted white leather doors and a tufted gray Ultrasuede headboard give the room a 1940s Hollywood star dressing room air. The soothing silvery grayness is interrupted by discreetly stunning modern art: Milton Avery's flesh-toned "Pink Dunes," Kenneth Noland's 105-inch-long "Untitled" acrylic and Niki de Saint-Phalle's somewhat brighter "Magic Bird."

"Style is a simple way of saying complicated things," declared Jean Cocteau, and White Hall proves his maxim. Displayed here are Bradfield's encyclopedic knowledge of art and decoration, his sensualist's penchant for lush textures and materials, his sense of restraint and class, his love of Hollywood's golden age and on and on. Yet not a bit of it is overwrought or outré, though it might easily have been. Together it provides the ages to come with as much to dissect as to learn from.

And, that is Bradfield's goal. "I believe that if one's work has resonance, it will outlive us," he says.

RIGHT: "I have always wanted to have a toile guest bedroom," says Bradfield, "but the subject matter was always too traditional…until now. This 'New York, New York' toile fitted my ideal of modernism perfectly." An abstract construction in painted wood and metal by Jesus Soto is placed on the night table. A portfolio of drawings by recognized Eastern Cape artist Margery Bradfield, the designer's sister, captures the survival spirit of Manhattan in the wake of September 11th.

"*The aim of art is living creation.*"

—*Joseph Albers*

OPENING PAGE: A formal allée of trees leads to the grand entrance of this
Georgian Revival estate. The Bentley GT is part of the client's collection
of exotic cars. Hanging in the limestone portico is a 19th-century copper,
brass and bronze lantern from the Rothschild estate that Bradfield
procured from B. Steintiz in Paris.

LEFT: Four Sam Francis acrylic paintings on canvas greet one just inside
the entrance hall and "climb the stair with one in a chic manner," says
Bradfield. The marble-floored corridor leads to the great room, past more
important art by Botero, Monet and others.

ABOVE: About halfway along this passage, Jean Dubuffet's "Mademoiselle
Neon" from 1948 hangs above an exceptional André Charles Boulle
console, "Préparation à la Danse, le Pied Droit en Avant" by Edgar Degas
and a pair of painted Neapolitan chairs.

If Nicolas Fouquet, Louis XIV's finance minister, were reincarnated as an American residing in Columbus, Ohio today, he might be someone resembling the gentleman who owns this grand residence. Like Fouquet, this entrepreneur (and his wife) required palatial digs to entertain on an impressive scale, both socially and as part of their extensive involvement in the philanthropic world. In his contemporary incarnation, however, the 17th-century figure would have acquired the wisdom of understatement.

Fouquet erected Vaux-le-Vicomte outside Paris, a chateau so glamorous that it landed him in some very hot water (the envious Sun King subjugated this panjandrum for raiding the treasury, then one-upped Fouquet's hubris by commissioning the building of Versailles). The present-day client, however, retained Bradfield to oversee and appoint an addition to expand the existing home, and it embodies a discretion Fouquet would have done well to observe.

Though the results are unquestionably luxurious, they also display a sense of humility and restraint, starting with the structure itself, which is built in the less affected American Georgian Revival style. While there's a certain grandeur to architect Don Goldstein's exterior stairways and terraces (they were inspired by those at The Mount, Edith Wharton's Lenox, Massachusetts estate), they bypass ostentation by being invisible from the approach, which reveals a much more sober and symmetrical brick façade at the end of a long allée of trees.

LEFT: The great room is visible at the end of the long entry corridor. In the foreground at left are the companion pieces to the Boulle console and painted Neapolitan chairs. Fernando Botero's "Maternity" bronze sculpture and Claude Monet's "Falaises et voiliers a Pourville" from 1882 are the artworks featured in this vignette.

> *"For me context is the key—from that comes the understanding of everything."*
>
> —Kenneth Noland

Yet, a hint that something more opulent awaits inside greets visitors at the limestone entry portico in the form of a finely cut 19th-century copper, brass and bronze lantern from the Rothschild estate, which Bradfield acquired for his clients at B. Steinitz in Paris. It is one of a pair (the other hangs in a rear loggia), and it perfectly conveys Bradfield's intentions for the interior of the home. "When I first started working for this family, their children were barely five years old," observes Bradfield. "The first home I did for them was simple and childproof. Eventually, it grew into this splendid 30,000-square-foot mansion."

That original collaboration was over 20 years ago, when the clients were budding collectors—"discerning and very acquisitive" in Bradfield's words. Arguably, the designer and architect's most ingenious concept for the newly expanded home was the addition of not one, but three, galleries that would accommodate the art and antiquities they have been consistently amassing since then. The galleries are grand affairs, in one case soaring to 24 feet in height and boasting antique mirrored walls, marble floors, custom-designed pilasters and moldings, and floor-to-ceiling etched glass cabinets.

PREVIOUS PAGES: The central focus of the great room is "Sound," a stunning Kenneth Noland target painting over the mantelpiece. The 19th-century French sconces flanking the fireplace, two of a set of eight, are gilded bronze and cut crystal and come from the Rothschild estate. The custom rug rests on 18th-century parquet de Versailles floors bordered in limestone. Bradfield designed the Ruhlmannesque coffee tables.

RIGHT: In a corner of the great room is a spectacular double-door cabinet acquired from B. Steinitz. It was made by Bernard van Risenburgh, an artist in Boulle's studio, circa 1700-10, of brass, ebony and tortoiseshell. A Lynn Chadwick sculpture sits on a console behind the sofa. The inlaid marble cocktail table is from Newel Galleries.

"The concept was so truly clear that we purchased many furnishings before we even broke ground," explains Bradfield. "I knew exactly where things were going to go." The aforementioned gallery, for example, cried out for two divans, which Bradfield also unearthed at B. Steinitz. The superb 19th-century mahogany examples by Georges-Alphonse Jacob Desmalter were just two of the many items Steinitz provided. Among others purchased for this space, Bradfield is particularly proud of two matching polychrome horn marquetry cabinets by André Charles Boulle, circa 1680. "Boulle was not fashionably sought-after back then; he was on the sidelines," notes Bradfield, who nevertheless recognized their importance immediately.

"There's not a lot of documentation of that period," says Benjamin Steinitz, even though there are pieces of Boulle's and another magnificent artist who worked in Boulle's studio, Bernard van Risenburgh, in the Louvre.

Steinitz acknowledges and praises Bradfield's acute eye. "He has a way of naturally reacting to quality that does not take into consideration the particular period from which an antique comes. His combinations are really exciting and creative. It's completely modern without being a clash." Steinitz refers to Bradfield, in fact, as a *chef d'orchestre*, for his ability to orchestrate harmonious interiors like a conductor.

LEFT: The paneling from Jean-Henri Jansen's masterpiece, his famous Madrid library, was the inspiration for this space, originally the home's living room. Bradfield had it executed in washed oak. Dubuffet's "Les Danseurs" hangs above the fireplace, paired with Diego Giacometti's "L'Autruche." In the foreground is Joan Miró's "Woman." The rare 19th-century Russian armchairs are mahogany and gilded wood.

The antique dealer cites the example of the first piece Bradfield and this client bought from him. "It was a fabulous Chinese armoire, something truly exceptional and of the rarest possible quality," Steinitz remembers. "Of course, it's gorgeous, and even though Chinese antiques were not being avidly collected at the time, they knew the quality of it. Mr. Bradfield set it in that wonderful long gallery, which is lightly toned. The effect of that warm wood, which is inset with brass and precious stones, is great. You have a modern setting with a piece that goes back to the 1600s." The armoire, he points out, eventually quadrupled in value.

Yet, lest one get the impression that Bradfield succumbed to the same grandiosity that did Fouquet in, he explains, "This project was never envisioned as a museum—always 'home' first." So, while the marble-floored gallery just inside the foyer is impressive—lined as it is with works by Monet and Botero—visitors eventually arrive in the great room to discover a sense of comfort and ease, immediately palpable. Rather than formal arrangements of straight-backed antique furniture, Bradfield chose roomy, luxuriantly upholstered sofas and armchairs that beckon visitors to sit and put their feet up. And the room is versatile in a way most great rooms are not: a screen descends from the ceiling, converting it instantly into a media room; excellent, says the wife, for watching Ohio State football games.

PREVIOUS PAGES: This gallery, the largest of three designed for the home, has 24-foot ceilings and features two superb circa 1815-30 Jacob divans from B. Steinitz, three 19th-century gilded bronze lanterns from the Rothschild estate and a pair of polychrome horn marquetry cabinets by Boulle.

RIGHT: Bradfield chose sapphire blue mohair walls in the dining room as a foil for Hans Hofmann's "Apparition" and a group of Marc Chagall paintings.

FOLLOWING PAGES: As in the great room, the dining room also features 18th-century parquet de Versailles floors bordered in limestone. Chagall's "Dans le Jardin" is flanked by 19th-century Guandong figures atop French, circa 1785, mahogany corner cupboards with chased gilded bronze ornament.

That is not to say the room doesn't traffic in important acquisitions. The most immediately apparent is "Sound," a stunning Kenneth Noland target painting of concentric circles. But its graphic quality does not detract from other rare finds. Among those are eight gilded bronze and rock crystal sconces from the Rothschild estate (the Steinitzes were friends of the Rothschilds and acquired "many things that were never on the market," says the dealer); a spectacular brass, ebony and tortoiseshell cabinet, circa 1700, by Bernard van Risenburgh; custom-designed Ruhlmannesque coffee tables, and custom carpets designed by Bradfield. All of these sit atop amazing 18th-century parquet de Versailles floors, also acquired from the venerable firm.

The expansions undertaken by Bradfield and the architect enabled his clients, he says, "to start collecting on a grand scale." The furnishings and objects, particularly an unparalleled collection of Judaica, are deployed throughout the large rooms with perfect taste and not a hint of ostentation. And, as always in Bradfield's projects, the world-class art informs much of the design. A series of Sam Francis paintings "climb the stair with one in a chic manner," says Bradfield. In the master bedroom, the gray-green colors of Dubuffet's 1954 painting "Paysage d'Été avec Vache" are echoed in the carpet and furniture. The landscape outside, essentially a work of natural art, contributes too; its view of mature forests comes indoors with a custom-designed iron bed boasting intertwined verdigris and white gold vines, and a custom carpet strewn with still more fallen leaves.

LEFT: In the master bedroom, Dubuffet's "Paysage d'Été avec Vache" proscribes the pale green color scheme. Below it is a Louis XVI wood console with a gris des Ardennes marble top, circa 1775, and two early 19th-century gilt painted Swedish chairs. Bradfield designed the rug by Stark Carpet, which takes its cue from the surrounding panorama of forest.

"In the animal world, Lalanne found an endless inventory of ideas. 'You don't have to explain what animals mean,' he said."

—The New York Times

In the dining room, Bradfield's cues came from Hans Hofmann's "Apparition" and a trio of bright Chagall paintings (now a quintet). His response? Walls upholstered in sapphire-blue mohair. "I wanted the dining room's story to be about the way the vibrant colors in the paintings appeared in that intensely blue room." The moral of that story is that they look magnificent.

Though everywhere one is reminded of Coco Chanel's pronouncement that "Luxury is a necessity that begins where necessity ends," the feeling of intimacy and comfort successfully avoids inspiring the sort of ire that Louis XIV felt toward Fouquet back in 1661. That is due to Bradfield's sensitive interpretation of his clients' desires and personalities. "These are honorable people, very civic minded," says Bradfield, who is currently at work, again consulting with architect Don Goldstein, on a temple for the family as well as collaborating on an apartment in Jerusalem. They use the residence not to impress, but to entertain friends and loved ones—crowds of them in fact—and to acknowledge the causes they hold dear. "Unlike the checkered history of Vaux-le-Vicomte, this home is infused with positive energy," observes Bradfield fondly. "The atmosphere is extraordinary."

RIGHT: An important table, "Troupeau d'Éléphants sous les Arbres" by François-Xavier Lalanne, is the fantastical centerpiece of a loggia that overlooks the swimming pool and tennis courts. The lantern is the second of a pair from the Rothschild estate; the other hangs in the entry portico. The chairs are jade green lacquer with gold trim.

"I call architecture frozen music."

—*Johann Wolfgang von Goethe*

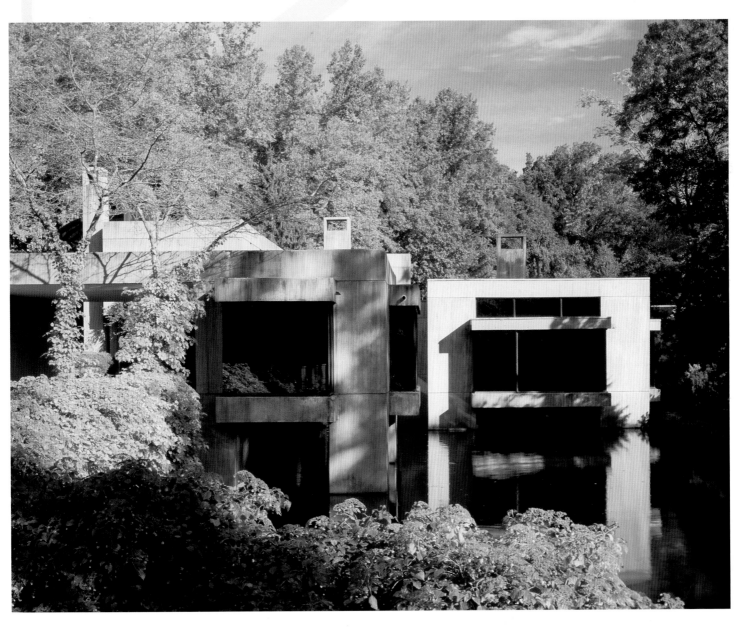

In 2007, Christie's called Bradfield with a special request. They were preparing to put the magnificent estate of Robin Roberts, founder in 1961 of the great fabric company Clarence House, on the block. "I had devised the concept for the Manhattan flagship and three other of his national showrooms," recalls Bradfield. "So they requested I create the design for the pre-sale installation." Bradfield undertook the job with enthusiasm, though undoubtedly also with some sadness, for Roberts's death had represented the loss of both friendship and a fine aesthetic mind.

Bradfield and his late business partner, the influential Jay Spectre, had been fast friends of Roberts and had collaborated on his spectacular modern country estate, a series of poured concrete buildings by architect Milton Klein in Bedford, New York. It was called Twin Ponds for the way the main house floated in and overlooked, à la Louis Kahn, a pair of serene catchments of water surrounded by lush gardens and forest.

OPENING PAGES: The Rateau chair (left), commissioned in 1919-20, recently sold at Christie's for $2 million. Architect Milton Klein designed poured concrete buildings cantilevered over water (right) for Robin Roberts's house, called Twin Ponds.

LEFT: The dramatic entrance features a circular Ruhlmann rug and an extraordinary silvered, gilt and patinated bronze jardinière by Edouard Marcel Sandoz, which is held aloft on a wrought iron stand by Edgar Brandt.

BELOW: In the entrance hall, Bradfield designed a brass compass eight-pointed star that was set into the marble floor below a Southeast Asian gilt, tin and paper-lined hall lantern. The Thuyawood stools were custom, and the lacquered screen, circa 1935, is by Pierre Bobot.

FOLLOWING PAGES: Over the living room fireplace is a Marcel Claude Renard gilt plaster maquette for a bridge ornament. The 19th-century Portuguese appliqué embroidered rug delineates a seating area that features sofas designed by Bradfield and Spectre, end tables by Ruhlmann (on left) and Süe et Mare (right). Atop the latter is an exquisite patinated bronze and alabaster lamp by Albert Cheuret.

"He was the most extraordinary man," remembers Bradfield. "Robin was one of those people who would never have anything in his house that wasn't absolutely impeccable. He revered unbelievable quality, and he was very dear to me, even though he was a prickly character. He gave me many gifts of appreciation that still give me great pleasure to this day."

Maurice Bernstein, an executor of Roberts's estate (whose idea it was to ask Bradfield to design the installation) concurs. "Even if Robin were buying a placemat," he says, "it had to be the perfect fabric, the perfect texture, the perfect color. He never compromised. I wanted to create the atmosphere of Twin Ponds at Christie's, and who better to do that than Geoffrey? He couldn't have been more gracious or wonderful."

Twin Ponds was not your typical casual country retreat. It was filled with exquisite furniture, objects and art. One needs no more evidence of this than the results of that legendary Christie's auction to underscore this point: It garnered more than double the highest presale expectations.

"The crown jewel in the collection would have to be the Rateau chair," Bradfield declares. The patinated bronze armchair, commissioned in 1919-20 by the collectors Florence and George Blumenthal for their Manhattan townhouse's indoor pool, fetched $2 million at the Christie's auction, and it exemplified the sort of provenance that pervaded the interiors at Twin Ponds. There, in the drawing room, it commanded a sublime view of the waterscapes and shared space with many other fine furnishings and objects.

Among these were "La Rhône et la Saône," a 1936 gilt plaster maquette for a bridge ornament by Marcel Claude Renard that hung over the fireplace; Donald Desky andirons; a pair of massive Qing Dynasty cabinets; side tables by Ruhlmann and by (Louis) Süe et (André) Mare; a beautifully crafted patinated bronze and alabaster lamp designed by Albert Cheuret in 1920; Jean Dunand nesting tables; "La Religieuse SN 31," a 1928 mahogany and alabaster floor lamp by Pierre Chareau that looks like an artistically abstracted nun in her wimple; and various upholstered pieces designed especially for the room, including a graphic zebra-patterned chaise.

To house all these museum-quality pieces without competing with the unbelievable sylvan panorama, Bradfield hit upon an ingenious concept. "Mother Nature was an amazing player in this project," Bradfield explains. So, the designers decided to "reinvent the forest materials inside, but in a high lacquer." Walls in almost every room were paneled in more exotic cousins of the wood on exhibit throughout the sculpted Armand Benedek-designed grounds. "You can't often use exotic woods the way we did," says Bradfield, explaining the extravagance of the look.

RIGHT: The Rateau chair shares the window with a Pierre Chareau floor lamp from the Hôtel du Tours.

Zebrawood imparted a luxe feeling to the entry, which showcased a stunning Edgar Brandt and Marcel Sandoz silvered, gilt and patinated bronze jardinière in the shape of a fish. Also greeting visitors in this entry were a gilt resin carp sculpture by François-Xavier and Claude Lalanne, a circular Ruhlmann rug, and two custom Thuyawood stools. The living room was upholstered in rich mohair velvet. The effect was like that of a movie theater. In this case, however, the plate glass windows with their spectacular views stood in for the silver screen.

In the dining room, Bradfield matched the walls to lacquered Macassar ebony chairs by Giovanni Michelucci, circa 1933. He also designed the Ruhlmannesque dining table of the same wood, and had it inlaid with ivory details. Silvered iron and glass consoles attributed to Raymond Subes also shared the space, while an alabaster and bronze Cheuret chandelier was suspended over the furnishings from a gold-leafed ceiling. A Raoul Dufy painting and a gilt nude sculpture by Alfred Janniot (first exhibited at the 1925 Exposition des Arts Decoratifs) surveyed the whole scene. The room was a Topkapi of rare treasures.

ABOVE: Framing the entrance to the dining room is the infamous patinated bronze relief created in 1930 by Charles Sargeant Jagger for London society figures Henry and Gwen Mond. "Scandal" depicted their early affair, which they shared with Gwen's lover, the poet Gilbert Cannan.

RIGHT: A detail of the couple kissing. The age difference between Henry and Gwen proved endless fodder for the local gossips. They met in 1918, when Henry, a prominent politician and businessman, crashed his motorcycle and was taken in by Gwen, then a young art student, and Cannan.

PREVIOUS PAGES: An important 1925 gilt plaster sculpture by Alfred Janniot (detail left) resembles a bather emerging from the surrounding ponds. She stands in the luxurious Macassar ebony-lined dining room (right) on a Süe et Mare carpet flanked by Raymond Subes consoles. The Giovanni Michelucci chairs from 1930 once belonged to Il Duce, the Italian dictator Benito Mussolini.

ABOVE: An ornate early 18th-century secretary with red and gilt-japanned finish is the impressive centerpiece of the library, which also includes circa 1801 Regency oak side chairs.

RIGHT: Above the fireplace hangs "Two Heads" by Jean Crotti. The red, black and gilt-japanned chandelier above the sofa is early 20th century. The entire room is paneled in richly lacquered zebrawood.

In the bedroom, a checkerboard pattern of lacquered bird's-eye maple rose behind the bed. Side tables displayed Diego Giacometti lamps. A 1940s Guglielmo Ulrich desk and chest of drawers, a lapis lazuli and steel Cartier clock, Roberto Matta candlesticks and a painting by Tchelitchew were a few of the precious items that were gathered here.

Of all the objects that sold at the Christie's auction that December, Bernstein is happiest about a patinated bronze relief by Charles Sargeant Jagger, circa 1930, called "Scandal." "I was very sad to dismantle Twin Ponds and sell everything that was so loved and cherished by Robin," he says. "I really wanted everything to find a good home, especially the Jagger, which went to the Victoria and Albert Museum in London."

Regarded as Jagger's most important decorative work, the sculpture depicted Henry and Gwen Mond, leading society figures of the day, whose ménage à trois with the poet Gilbert Cannan had raised eyebrows in 1918. It was a highbrow slap in the face to the gossip that had run rampant throughout London at the time. So it was an incredibly intimate story set out into the world for everyone to see.

In many respects, Twin Ponds was Robin Roberts's version of "Scandal," a highly personal statement about who he was, albeit a less scandalous one. "It was his life's work," says Bradfield with affection.

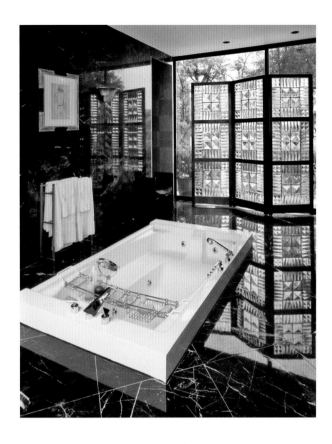

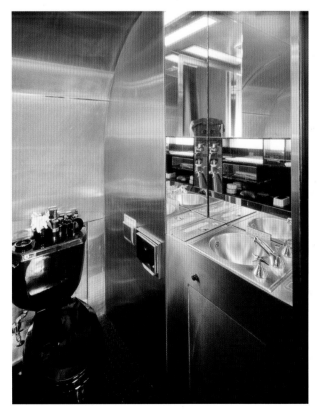

LEFT: In the master bedroom, Guglielmo Ulrich's elegantly tapered palmwood, ebony and shagreen desk overlooked lush woodland. It was paired with an anonymous silvered wood Deco chair.

RIGHT TOP: The breathtakingly simple black marble master bath had a tub sunken into the floor. A three-paneled glass screen provided privacy without blocking available light.

RIGHT BOTTOM: A sleek powder room, clad in stainless steel, its curved walls and recessed lighting creating the impression of one being in the fuselage of an airplane.

"*Art is the signature of civilizations.*"

—*Beverly Sills*

"An ambassador is not simply an agent; he is also a spectacle."

—*Walter Bagehot*

The Kingdom of Morocco gained its independence in 1956. But, the style that pervaded its days as a French Protectorate lives on elegantly at the New York residence of Morocco's Ambassador to the United Nations. It is the sort of mansion that one imagines would be occupied by diplomats conducting delicate negotiations over famous international contretemps. The interiors designed for the home by Bradfield heed the observation of Victorian economist, editor and political analyst Walter Bagehot: "An ambassador is not simply an agent; he is also a spectacle."

OPENING PAGES: Detail of a beaded peacock lamp gracing the master suite.

PREVIOUS PAGES: The impressive entry to the Moroccan Embassy, Bradfield says, "has a strong Robert Adam reference." The custom screen design was based on the shape of a Moorish scimitar.

LEFT: The second-floor landing provides access to two reception rooms. Here, two 18th-century French chairs—two more are visible in the reception room beyond—flank a Gilbert Poillerat console. A Lynn Chadwick sculpture sits on the console.

ABOVE: Peering down the grand, winding stairwell at this landing from several floors above.

> *"The Moroccan lifestyle is evident in the costumes of the staff, the tagines and the rose petals strewn on the table."*
>
> —Geoffrey Bradfield

Spectacle depends heavily on stagecraft, and in that department Bradfield's competitors are few. But stagecraft must have a connection to something of great substance if it is to endure. Of course, substance certainly flows from the sheer presence of the townhouse's ambassadorial inhabitants. But this distinguished Upper East Side address also came with an indisputable pedigree: the five-storey, 8,000-square-foot home was built by John H. Duncan (of Grant's Tomb) in 1899 for Benjamin Guggenheim, father of art patron extraordinaire Peggy Guggenheim. It is sited on the same block as spectacular mansions designed by C.P.H. Gilbert for luxury furnishings magnate Henry T. Sloane, and gas mogul Oliver Gould Jennings. Recently another important fuel and gas power moved onto the block next door to the Moroccan embassy; it is now the United States home of the Emir of Qatar.

At the turn of the century, Guggenheim's house embodied its own opulent spectacle, filled as it was with tiger skin rugs and Louis XVI furniture. That laconically posh existence came to a tragic end in 1912, when Benjamin went down with the Titanic. That the Treaty of Fez, which established the French Protectorate in Morocco, was signed that very same year is a bizarre coincidence when considered from the perspective of the manse's current incarnation.

PREVIOUS PAGES: This reception room is distinguished by a sumptuous 19th-century rug and 18-foot ceilings framed by restored, regilded moldings. There are three seating areas, one with a pair of custom fringed banquettes flanking a fireplace (left), round Diego Giacometti tables and a Poillerat coffee table; the other a large custom sofa against a mirrored wall (right), juxtaposed with two 18th-century French chairs and a pair of Poillerat consoles.

LEFT: Two Chinese 18th-century carved cinnabar palace vases and chairs lacquered in the same hue create drama in the dining room.

ABOVE: The table is set with silver tagines and the royal china, crystal and cutlery.

Bradfield's bifurcated approach to the project was to re-establish the old structural grandeur of the historic property (the marble floors and staircases, for example, were completely restored) and to give the residence a contemporary context. Today, clean open rooms feel simultaneously modern and stately. The foyer is a very formal space that immediately proclaims its monarchy. "I used peacock blue here because it exhibits a regal message," says Bradfield. "It has a very strong Adam reference," he adds, speaking of the 18th-century Neoclassical Scottish architect Robert Adam, who was responsible for many of England's great houses.

Regal peacock blue is rendered in the woven runner that climbs the stair and in room screens crowned with a Moroccan motif that Bradfield adapted, he explains, "from the shape of a Moorish scimitar." Traces of it also run through the pair of Louis XV chairs upholstered in tapestry fabric that flank an 18-century Dutch console. A lapis lazuli tile border defines the entry, beyond which ornate iron gates lead down a flight of gracious stairs to a dining room, a cinnabar fantasia anchored by a grandly scaled, intricately woven Oriental carpet from the Ambassador's collection.

In this room, Bradfield dispatches Gallic glamour by regilding the boiserie trim in a muted gold. A French chandelier and two octagonal Venetian mirrors preside over a room pulsating with the flame red hue: the dining chairs are lacquered with it, and two 18th-century carved Chinese vases also boast this vivid color. The table is set with the royal service, which includes exquisite silver tagines that make clear the Moroccan lifestyle conducted within the walls of the mansion. "It is evident in the costumes of the staff and the rose petals strewn on the table," says Bradfield.

LEFT: Walnut boiserie gives the Ambassador's library, which is in the private quarters, a sense of comfort and warmth. The armillary globe and elephant tables are from Newel Galleries.

Muted gold is used on the boiserie trim of majestic reception rooms on the second floor as well, where ceilings soar to 18 glorious feet. Pendulous chandeliers drip with crystals over another sumptuous 19th-century rug that Bradfield says is "the soul of the room." French 1940s furniture signifies the height of Gallic influence in North Africa. Fine examples here include Gilbert Poillerat consoles and a coffee table as well as an impossibly superb set of four 18th-century French armchairs that are elaborately carved, gilded and upholstered, again, in peacock blue velvet (the latter from the estate of designer-collector Michael Greer, who had one of the largest private collections of Empire and Directoire furniture in the world). Moroccan paintings depicting ancient medina walls of the country's royal cities and princely stables, a contemporary sculpture by British artist Lynn Chadwick and exotically patterned Bergamo fabric on custom upholstered chairs complete the cultural mix.

More private quarters such as the library and master bedroom also exhibit a flair that draws equally from either side of the Straits of Gibraltar. The library, for example, is paneled in handsome walnut boiserie and houses a major Moroccan painting depicting medina residents perched on the red clay battlements of a desert city. In the bedroom the mix more strongly favors the North African side of the equation. Two incredibly ornate mother-of-pearl inlay chairs flank a Gilbert Poillerat side table with a lapis lazuli top. On it are colored crystal peacock lamps from Newel Galleries. Even the bed throw, though by American designer Donna Karan, is patterned and embroidered with a design that evokes North African textiles.

"It is the absolute antithesis of the Bedouin tented city," says Bradfield of the Moroccan Embassy, more in the spirit of international Tangier or Casablanca than tribal desert caravan. "There are very few legitimate kings left in the world," he adds wistfully. This majestic residence ensures that when in town on official business, at least one of these crowned heads can entertain in a place befitting his station.

RIGHT: Exceedingly ornate Syrian ebony chairs with mother-of-pear inlay (flanking a Gilbert Poillerat table), the beaded peacock lamps and an Eastern-inspired throw by Donna Karan bring exotic touches to the master suite.

"*The job of the artist is always to deepen the mystery.*"

—*Francis Bacon*

Ramón Emilio Jimenez should have been a matador. Like Tyrone Power playing Juan Gallardo in *Blood and Sand*, or a young Robert Evans in his role as Pedro Romero in *The Sun Also Rises*, Jimenez cuts a dark, dashing figure. "He loves bullfighting," says Bradfield. "He's a man's man, but he recognizes beauty; a sophisticated gentleman from a Dominican patrician family who knows how to live." Jimenez, a charter member of Casa de Campo, is the sort of bon vivant who skis in Gstaad, splashes around the beaches of Saint-Tropez and shoots wild fowl in the Toledo countryside. And of course, "he's absolute catnip for women," says Bradfield.

OPENING PAGES: Bradfield's concepts (left) for the drawing room rug, inspired by Spanish metalwork, and the glorious result (right).

THESE PAGES: A rendering of the drawing room layout (left), and the finished space (right), with Julio Larraz's painting "A Comedy of Power" above the console.

FOLLOWING PAGES: A pair of signed Jansen bérgères give the room historical heft. The table, carpet and sectional sofa were custom designed by Bradfield. Uruguayan artist Pablo Atchugarry's marble sculpture is at right.

PABLO ATCHUGARRY

Their meeting was serendipitous. Jimenez, in the market for a New York pied-à-terre, came to see an apartment Bradfield was selling on East 62nd Street some years ago. "It was too small for him, but he loved the décor," recounts Bradfield. "He said that when he found a place, it was I who would design it."

Jimenez stayed true to his word, calling Bradfield as soon as he purchased an amply proportioned one-bedroom on Park Avenue. "He's different from other designers," says the Latin mogul, "Geoffrey has a very high level of sensitivity, and it shows in his work."

One needs no further evidence of that sensitivity than the deft and subtle way in which Bradfield weaves in references to Jimenez's ancestry. His client has an important Latin American art collection that would figure prominently, of course. But, explains Bradfield, "He wanted the apartment to be very international in style. You could put this apartment down in any capital of the world."

THESE PAGES: Different views of the drawing room, with its desk-cum-dining table in a recessed corner. The flat-screen television is concealed behind mirrored glass panels that blend into the wall.

In the drawing room the designer showcased "A Comedy of Power," a painting by Cuban artist Julio Larraz, and a marble sculpture by Uruguayan Pablo Atchugarry amid a global and epochal salmagundi of styles: Jansen bérgères, a contemporary custom sectional sofa, a French Deco-style coffee table and a console made from the lyre-shaped bases of two Robsjohn-Gibbings tables (which Bradfield regilded in white gold). Underfoot is the *pièce de résistance*, a deeply carved oval custom rug that echoes the sinuous metalwork of ornate Spanish railings and gates one sees throughout the grand residences of South America and the Caribbean. The rug is stylized so classically that its Iberian-Hispanic inflection, while certainly clear—and clearly gorgeous—nevertheless remains an exquisite understatement.

ABOVE: Hammered silver vases atop a console comprised of two Robsjohn-Gibbings bases.

RIGHT: The white porcelain table lamp with Neoclassical figures is one of a pair acquired from Salibello. The silver bull sculpture was a gift from Bradfield to his client.

"He's a man's man, but he recognizes beauty; a sophisticated gentleman from a Dominican patrician family who knows how to live."

—Geoffrey Bradfield

There are also Neoclassical Art Moderne lamps on Deco side tables, as well as a French table and Gustavian chairs in one corner that serve double duty as desk and romantic dining area. Squares of mirror cover the wall behind, two of them opening to reveal a cleverly concealed flat-screen television. It would be hard to get more international than this.

The bedroom is a playboy's plush lair, completely outfitted in Jimenez's favorite color: French blue. Bradfield had doors and bedside tables upholstered in blue Ultrasuede and leather, then spectacularly trimmed with a nailhead pattern that recalls "the Alhambra in Spain," says Bradfield. Yet, like the rug in the drawing room, the pattern is so handsomely stylized, the sheer luxury of its nickel-plated nail-head trim so spellbinding, that these items stand on their own luxe character whether one perceives the Spanish reference or not.

PREVIOUS AND THESE PAGES: The master suite is a nailhead-trimmed Ultrasuede and leather rhapsody in French blue, the client's favorite color. Julio Larraz's painting "The Velasquez Room" dominates one wall. Berrocal's "Mini David" sculpture complements an Art Deco side table.

Bradfield set up an intimate interaction between this bed and another that is the subject matter of the Larraz painting, "The Velasquez Room." The latter is occupied by a languidly rendered nude. Her curvaceous form is in turn echoed in the voluptuous silhouette of a Venetian filigree desk. The room perfectly balances the feminine and the masculine. And both aspects converge with unqualified refinement in the bedside lamps Bradfield found at Pascal Boyer Gallery. Their shapes resemble abstracted steer heads—another bullfighting reference—yet the horns are fragile crystal, and the taurine "head" is gilded bronze. "The room is about visual seduction," says Bradfield, and one believes him implicitly.

The same could be said of the entire pied-à-terre. For anyone, whether male or female, the colors, textures and art here are as fascinating and alluring as the passion of a bullring.

LEFT: The nickel-plated nailhead trim on the headboard and side table recalls motifs in palaces like the Alhambra. The gilded bronze and crystal bull lamps were a serendipitous, and synchronous, find from Pascal Boyer Gallery.

BELOW: A plasma screen television in the master bedroom is recessed above a 19th-century Venetian filigree table from Newel Galleries.

"Beauty is like God; a fragment of beauty is complete…"

— *Auguste Rodin*

If White Hall, Bradfield's classically stylish townhouse, reveals the designer to be a man who deftly juggles propriety and panache, his Park Avenue garçonnière just around the corner indulges his voluptuary side. White Hall, of course, serves as both office and entertaining space for large parties and promotions, as well as a showcase for prospective clients. So, it is natural that it manifests his more public persona.

Bradfield's "escape hatch," on the other hand, displays a plush and joyous free reign that is grounded by his use of classical sculpture. "When I want to be alone, or alone with a friend, I escape to the flat," says Bradfield. "It's a self-contained island of serenity."

Perched on a high floor, with views of a white church cupola and a Gothic spire ("It's as close to Florence as you can get in Manhattan," he says), it exudes "unapologetic glamour—the world of Hollywood movies from the '30s—those shimmering mirages of penthouse high life. My aim here was to create the same kind of all-out seduction in miniature."

Woe to the one being seduced...resistance is futile! Luscious textures abound. There is shimmering satin on two French Art Moderne slipper chairs purchased in Paris, and on a Louis XV settee from Christie's—the latter's lavishly curvaceous form dominating the room with the fearless confidence of youthful beauty. Acrylic consoles and a "Sabre" bench by Bradfield, as well as an Essey of Denmark acrylic table, have a sexy, bare-it-all transparency. White metals—platinum-leaf detailing on the pilasters (a Bradfield architectural addition), chrome twig sconces and the silvery frames of the chairs and settee—tease the light playfully, engaging it and reflecting it like the lamé of a starlet's evening gown. And, mirrors all around, while visually expanding the space beyond its physical constraints, lend a touch of coquettishness.

Scale also plays a brazen role in Bradfield's seduction. Like a lothario's outsized self-assurance, over-scaled art and objects announce their presence with no self-consciousness whatsoever. Tam Ochiai's "Elisabeto," an enormous oil and graphite on canvas, takes up most of a wall. Bradfield's cut-pile silk rug boasts gigantic acanthus leaves that would be at home in the torrid hothouse environment of a tropical forest. And in the bedroom, Bradfield blew up a detail from Tiepolo's "Departure of the Gondola" and used it to cover the walls. The image of liveried footmen envelops the room to create, he says, "a dream-like atmosphere." Mirror behind the bed and on the closet doors reflects these attendants endlessly. "I go to sleep like a Venetian prince," Bradfield says only half in jest, "surrounded by footmen and under a crucifix."

Of course, this kind of luxury could have tripped disastrously into hedonism. "I love luxury," admits Bradfield, "but not when it's superfluous." He averts self-indulgence by punctuating the two-room apartment with classical sculpture. These add gravitas and, poignantly, function like the vanitas paintings of the Renaissance to remind us of our mortality and of the ephemeral nature of existence. "The head of a goddess on the coffee table, the torso of Asclepius on a pedestal, the marble nude of a hero on my desk," explains Bradfield. "These are relics that transcend the decorative. They inspired worship millennia ago, and still do. As Borromini put it, 'The Greek and Roman religions have long since gone, and a large part of our own will go someday, but what is lost for faith is retained for beauty.' The secret is to find a balance between wit and sincerity. The masters who chiseled these classical figures, and paid homage to the eternal in them, help keep one pure of heart."

Naturally, Bradfield's humility for the eternal only serves to make the surroundings here even more alluring, ensuring the temptation is deliciously complete. After all, piety mixed with eros is a strong aphrodisiac (just consider the long line of womanizing popes that extends from Sergius III to Alexander VI). Why bother to resist?

"I love luxury, but not when it's superfluous."

—Geoffrey Bradfield

OPENING PAGES: An intimate impromptu supper (left) is set up in the apartment's mirrored entry hall. Custom Italian twig sconces above a Bradfield-designed console (right), which is topped with rare Olympic marble.

SECOND SPREAD: Tam Ochiai's "Elisabeto" dominates a wall in the living room near the Greek 2nd-century draped torso of Asclepius from Fortuna Fine Arts.

THIRD SPREAD: On the custom overscaled acanthus leaf carpet, a Louis XV settee from Christie's and two Art Moderne chairs surround a customized Joan Sherman White Branch table.

TOP: Mirrored panels framed by classical pilasters visually expand the space.

RIGHT: A silver Lynn Chadwick sculpture on the Essey of Denmark acrylic table is juxtaposed with a marble 2nd-century Roman bust of a goddess.

FOLLOWING PAGES: Bradfield blew up "Tiepolo's Departure of the Gondola" and deployed it as wall covering in the bedroom.

LAST PAGES: Jeff Koons's "Balloon Dog" (left) rests beside the bed. A cupola and a Gothic spire are visible outside the window behind a 1st-century marble torso of a Roman hero.

"Painters must speak through paint,
not through words..."

—Hans Hofmann

"No decade of the 20th century had such a distinctive flavor and legendary atmosphere as the 1920s," avers Bradfield. "One cannot underestimate the importance of the Art Deco period on our lifestyle and how we perceive our interiors today." Its influence was compounded, he adds, "mainly because of the emerging movie industry, which used it to exemplify sophistication and wealth. Because of this medium, we are led to believe that it was 'mass' production, but indeed it was not."

It was the age of white dinner jackets, square-shouldered satin peignoirs, the Chrysler and Empire State buildings, the sleek ocean liner and the streamline Zephyr train. And because "one associates Deco with the metropolis, with Manhattan," says Bradfield, a 1920s-30s aesthetic was the obvious choice for a project he undertook in the 1990s: the renovation of and addition to a pre-war Upper East Side penthouse.

"It was the first project I did for our firm from beginning to end; Jay gave me carte blanche," says Bradfield of his late partner, Jay Spectre. The team had designed this couple's Westchester mansion, a far more traditional affair. But, for this pied-à-terre, the clients longed for a departure that would match the polish and suave strut of the city. It would not come easily, Bradfield recalls: "The original living room had not been touched in 30 years. We knocked down walls where we could, gutted the entire space and made it more open-plan. There were no rules."

OPENING PAGES: The media room's walls are upholstered in dark green mohair, dramatically setting off "Red Faces," by Hans Hofmann.

LEFT: Leo Raiken's 1937 "Granite Quarry" hangs above a Macassar ebony Ruhlmann cabinet in the drawing room.

Daunting enough for a young designer, to be sure. But, the clients also required more space, so Bradfield negotiated with the Landmarks Preservation Commission to win approval of a new master suite with a wraparound terrace that would be built on the rooftop of the building. Joining these two floors turned out to be one of Bradfield's most dazzling maneuvers. A brushed steel and Macassar ebony staircase that looks transported from the Normandie itself rises from the entrance hall to the private quarters. At the top, a separate glass door allows guests access to the terrace without having to traverse the master suite, while it also floods the stairwell with light.

Bradfield reconfigured rooms, erecting walls that he covered in supple raw silk. A palette of ebony, taupe and beige unifies the spaces and serves as a tasteful backdrop for WPA-era art and some outstanding Deco furniture, as well as custom-designed pieces that bring the period look up to date. The exception to the monochromatic rule is the media room. "The colors are very vivid, the graphics borderline graffiti," says Bradfield. "I always find it exciting to look from a restrained four walls into a fiery other room." The walls there are "British racing green mohair velvet," and they throw Hans Hofmann's 1945 painting "Red Faces" into dramatic relief. The luscious fabric also serves to soften the acoustics.

ABOVE: A custom-designed, Deco-style formal staircase of Macassar ebony and brushed steel unites the two floors.

RIGHT: Above a custom brushed steel and granite console is Thomas Hart Benton's "Water Story," circa 1929. The media room is visible beyond.

"One cannot underestimate the importance of the Art Deco period on our lifestyle and how we perceive our interiors today."

—Geoffrey Bradfield

Bradfield collaborated with his clients to collect works by Thomas Hart Benton, Alexander Archipenko, Leo Raiken and other artists of the 1930s, many from the Michael Rosenfeld Gallery, which specialized in the era. Industrial working-class scenes like Raiken's "Granite Quarry," Guy Wiggins's "Ivorytown Plant" and Benton's "Water Story" provide a counterpoint to Lalique and Bouley vases, a divine inlaid Macassar ebony cabinet attributed to Ruhlmann and other fine objects. These paintings remind us that Art Deco was concurrent with the Great Depression and, in this way, serve as forerunners to Bradfield's propensity for balancing ephemeral luxury with art and furnishings that bring relativity and emotional weight to the design.

In fact, Bradfield says, "There is a strong influence of Eugène Printz in this apartment; modernism intimately linked with functionalism." Many of Printz's furniture designs, while luxurious in their materials, had an angular practicality to them that predated the Bauhaus austerity that was to come. That functionalism here conveys a Deco glamour tethered to American pragmatism and blue-collar values. It is the means by which Bradfield elegantly avoids all pretension.

LEFT: The dining room is elegant, yet informal, featuring a comfortable banquette and art by Alexander Archipenko and Guy Wiggins.

"I'm looking for the unexpected. I'm looking for things I've never seen before."

—Robert Mapplethorpe

Purples signify many things: bravery, valor, a certain style of ornate prose. Douglas Lloyd, principal of the company that designed violet ads for Estée Lauder's Sensuous fragrance, chose the color, he recently told *Time* magazine, based on "its royal connotations, a richness that conjures the idea of religion and incense."

Yet, few designers have tackled purple in interiors, notes Bradfield, except as an accent color. He remembers some of those more intrepid souls: "Its last big impact was in the '60s," he recalls. "Mary Quant used it with orange. David Hicks used it with green. Yves Saint Laurent turned purple and olive into the great fashion fusion."

Bradfield's own opportunity to explore the many shades of purple arose when he was asked to design this Manhattan apartment. Because of the owner's violet tendencies, he knew he would need to plunder its spectrum—from pale lilac to plum—and invent a few other shades along the way.

Subscribing fearlessly to the schools of Quant, Hicks and Saint Laurent, Bradfield took up the challenge. But, he chose to cleave to the more understated, up-to-date sophistication that dwells at the paler end of the spectrum, achieving variety by unearthing a startling array of textural contrasts. In doing so, he bowled over the owner of this glamorous 4,000-square-foot duplex at 500 Park Avenue, an award-winning building designed by Skidmore Owings & Merrill, overlooking Central Park. "I was so moved," says the client. "I couldn't believe he could find so many fabrics in my color. And, he brought me variations on a theme, not repetition."

OPENING PAGES: Helen Frankenthaler's awe-inspiring "Crete" is the backdrop for a corner vignette in the drawing room. "Dan" by Boaz Vaadia is on the coffee table.

SECOND SPREAD: Among the objects gathered in the living room is a spectacular aluminum and black lacquer baby grand piano and French bérgères lacquered in vivid pink.

RIGHT: Louise Nevelson's black "Column" at left is a strong presence in an otherwise soothing anegré-paneled room with accents of ice blue, mauve and hot pink.

The client was already predisposed to Bradfield's style; a visit to another home he had decorated some time before had made a marked impression. That first encounter with the designer's work, she recalls, was transformative. "Seeing that room was like hearing the Beatles for the first time."

Her apartment came with some distinct disadvantages: an awkward layout of disparate, low-ceilinged rooms spread over two floors, and no unifying elements to tie them together. Architect Gavin Macrae-Gibson reconfigured those spaces, opening everything up to light and views. Walls on both floors are swathed in book-matched fiddleback anegré wood paneling. The spaces still needed to be connected and a coherent dialogue between them established. To this end, a brushed stainless-steel staircase was designed and carpeted in a purple-striped runner that referenced the palette of lavenders Bradfield had mixed for the rooms.

ABOVE: The dining room boasts an Italian smoked mirror-and-giltwood table surrounded by Art Moderne Réné Prou chairs.

RIGHT: The room's focal point is a graphic surrealistic painting called "Paysage Imaginaire" by Jean Metzinger.

The floor-to-ceiling richness of the anegré went a long way toward dissimulating the low overhead space, mesmerizing the eye with its verticality to make ceilings appear higher. Bradfield went still further, performing a clever sleight of hand: in the drawing room, he hung vertically striped Bergamo Roman shades from the very tops of the windows, creating the illusion that they continue above the soffets. In the bedroom, a bolder vertical stripe from Scalamandré achieves the same effect. And, to fool the eye into believing the ceiling above is 12 rather than nine feet, he kept furnishings deep and low-slung.

When it came to color, Bradfield realized that too much purple passion could easily devolve into purple perversity. "Purple can be a very carnal color, and not for the faint of heart," he explains. "It has to be used with economy, and it has to be balanced with other colors to achieve its full contribution."

Nothing plays a more prominent role here in breaking up the violet haze than art. Most breathtaking is a gigantic salmon and brown Helen Frankenthaler painting called "Crete." The work was so large, recalls Bradfield, it had to be taken off the stretcher and rolled up, then re-stretched on site. The Frankenthaler, with all the complication that attended its installation, is an uncannily apt painting for the space. The artist tended to dilute her pigments heavily with turpentine or kerosene, giving them the more subtle quality, like Miró or Diebenkorn, of "washes" of color. This subtlety of values works perfectly with the muted shades of purple Bradfield deployed throughout the apartment.

It also oddly mirrors the delicate calibration of Bradfield's technique. "When a picture looks labored and overworked," explained Frankenthaler years ago, "and you can read in it—well, she did this and then she did that, and then she did that—there is something in it that has not got to do with beautiful art to me. One really beautiful wrist motion, that is synchronized with your head and heart, and you have it. It looks as if it were born in a minute."

That is exactly the impression one gets of this room. It looks like, in Frankenthaler's words, "an immediate image," as if it sprung—without hint of the difficulty of its creation, transport and installation—fully realized, like Athena springing fully grown from the head of Zeus. Like all of Bradfield's work, it appears to come together effortlessly.

LEFT: The dining room table set for dinner with a Ming Dynasty terra cotta figurine as a centerpiece.

Other artworks that serve to modulate the purple reign include a totemic black Louise Nevelson construction, "Column," and "Dan," a small bronze and stone statue by Boaz Vaadia. They inject darker, rougher contrasts into the sea of pastels. In the dining room, the reds, blacks, ivories and blues of a Jean Metzinger painting add a graphic punch to vanilla Venetian plaster walls trimmed in more anegré. And, a deep blue, stunningly gestural Sam Francis work in the master bedroom is both a pause in the parade of purples and—in blue's position as half the component hues that comprise this color—a reinforcement of it.

Also adding heft to a palette that could threaten to float away on a breeze are elegantly proportioned antiques, the most striking a pair of unusual French 1940s Neoclassical bérgères, found at B. Steinitz in Paris, lacquered by Leo Huillard in daring hot pink. They share space with a coolly elegant aluminum-and-black lacquer baby grand piano, a steel and bronze marble-topped side table from the Georges V Hotel in Paris, and a voluptuously curvaceous Italian mirrored coffee table near the Frankenthaler. A 1940s Italian smoked mirror and gilded dining table, and a large mirrored and etched commode in the dining room perform the same service.

Purple "traces its roots back to kings and cardinals," the same *Time* article informs us. "In the days when thousands of mollusks had to be crushed to make a single drop of purple dye, a process only those with legions of servants could afford." Thankfully, that process is less arduous today. With so many tints and shades to choose from, Bradfield allowed himself to have tremendous fun. "To my surprise, I found myself enjoying integrating this unfamiliar palette into the space," he says. An enjoyment that is passionately purple.

LEFT: A gestural Sam Francis painting in the master bedroom pulls out the bluer hues of the purple palette. Bradfield designed the carpet, with its simulated basketweave pattern.

"*I just wanted to find out where the boundaries were. I've found out there aren't any.*"

—Damien Hirst

Every artist at one point in his or her career creates an homage to his age. It could be said that this white-glove, L-shaped New York apartment is Bradfield's paean to the preternaturally inspired 1970s. It was designed, in fact, for a young couple he met when the decade was reaching its zenith.

"I arrived in New York in 1977," says Bradfield. "It was absolutely the perfect time to move here...brilliant! It was a period of such total confidence—the Bee Gees' music, Studio 54 night after night, Regine's, Doubles, Le Club and Elmo's per kind favor of Ludovic Autet's JICs (Junior International Club). Baryshnikov had just jumped ship and was on the cover of *Time*. My first Thanksgiving here was spent with Mary McFadden at the peak of her celebrity. It was a miraculous moment, and so ephemeral in a way."

The apartment's current incarnation deliriously conjures the era's genie from its bottle. The miracle of this project is that, while the '70s references are identifiably intact, the whole collage of its ingredients is not at all dated. Bradfield has interpreted ideas that first took root in the kinetic days of Warhol and the Factory and fast-forwarded them to the next millennium. In fact, there is a futuristic mood to things here.

Take, for instance, the way black lacquer and the Japanese influence were incorporated into interiors back then—too much of the former and lack of nuance in application of the latter led to rooms that often looked slick or faux Asian. Black lacquer has its presence here too, but it is measured. And, Bradfield tweaks an iconic Japanese staple, the shoji screen, riffing on it cleverly in a custom rug that he installs on the diagonal. The trick instantly expands the space. "It's all about illusion," explains Bradfield. "Because of the diagonal you really feel there is far more volume to the space."

OPENING PAGES: Bradfield grounded the room with a custom rug (left) sporting an abstracted grid that echoes the surrounding windows and the mirrored shoji screens. A dress sculpture by Sophie De Francesca (right) approaches "Ghost Tree [Malevich]," a wall-mounted piece by Katy Stone.

SECOND SPREAD: The baby sculpture atop the 1960s Roberto Gabetti table from Karl Kemp is by the Luo Brothers. The diagonal pattern on the rug creates the illusion of a larger volume.

LEFT: "Dripping," a painting by Hideaki Kawashima, hovers above a custom sectional sofa. Nicola Bolla's crystal-covered "Puma" below.

A wall of authentic shoji runs between living and dining areas. Its traditional paper has been replaced by mirror, continuing the play, while also serving to conceal storage for the dinner china and services. The prevalence of grids (recurring on the windows) establishes geometric order at the same time that it skews one's sense of the room's shape and configuration. And just to throw us another curve, Bradfield deployed a 1960s Roberto Gabetti dining table. The black palisander and tubular chrome pedestal appears to pick up a strand of one of the rug's delineations and take it for a sensual joy ride.

The art here also sustains connections to a fascinating era without pandering to it. "It's eminently daring," says Bradfield of the collection. It's hard to look at Nicola Bolla's 2005 Swarovski crystal-skinned "Puma," for example, without also contemplating the mirrored ball and its place in 1970s disco culture. Yet, Bradfield faces it off with a 14th-century Venetian lion, injecting tension and timelessness that swings it far away from glitz or kitsch. The Luo Brothers' sculpture of a mischievous babe atop a hamburger, though dating only to 2007, would never have been possible without Warhol's Pop Art ironies. ("It astounded me," says the client of the piece. "It screamed 'Buy me!' And every time I look at it, it makes me smile.")

RIGHT: "Puma" faces off with a Venetian lion sculpture from the 14th century. In the background is "Marked Trees," an oil on canvas by Hugo Bastidas.

The Japanese ukiyo-e prints that were all the rage back in the day are replaced with art that has an up-to-the-second relevance: "Dripping," a manga-inspired acrylic on canvas by Hideaki Kawashima, looks over the leonine confrontation. A sexy disembodied dress made of galvanized wire mesh by Sophie De Francesca seems to approach "Ghost Tree" [Malevich]," an acrylic, Duralor and nylon wall-mounted sculpture by Katy Stone. The selections are edgy and alive in a consummately contemporary way. There's no sense at all of being in some sort of time capsule.

"Geoffrey has a great eye when it comes to art," says the gallery owner Nohra Haime, "and not only 20th-century masters, but also younger artists. He's willing to take chances."

In fact, if anything is responsible for creating the youthful vigor the apartment exudes, it is a collection of painting and sculpture that includes emerging artists, with all the experimentation and originality that implies. And, they are cheek-by-jowl with the work of their better-known brethren. "What is fascinating," says Haime, "is when these young artists can stand next to more established artists. It shows that they will go far. It's not a question of age, but more of quality."

"All beautiful things belong to the same age," says Bradfield, borrowing from Wilde.

His client couldn't agree more. "The apartment turned out to be a fantasy for us," she enthuses. "Each piece we chose is special in its own right, and each one belongs exactly where it is." That is, with one foot in the 1970s and another in 2025. In our art-directed world of today, here Bradfield has broken free from the pack and stirred up an inimitable formula and flair for cosmopolitan living.

RIGHT: A Karl Springer table and Bradfield's award-winning "Coco" chair rest on a custom cantaloupe and ivory "cracked ice" rug. Jim Dine's "Dutch Hearts" is on the wall beyond.

"There are no rules. That is how art is born."

—Helen Frankenthaler

In a bygone era, one could say "English gentleman" and it was clear exactly what that meant. He was Wodehouse's man-about-town, Bertie Wooster, attended by his faithful valet, Jeeves. Independently wealthy, schooled at Eton, well mannered, dining at his private club and possessing, perhaps, a bit of the rake. This character has become a rarity amidst a fast-paced world that often does not recognize the value of gentility. English gentleman today can mean something more substantial—someone less attached to Empire, jetting around the world not on a Grand Tour, but on high-powered business trips and exclusive vacations in the Mediterranean.

The man who owns this Manhattan residence exists somewhere in between these two understandings of the English gentleman. Bradfield points out that, like eminent Victorians and Edwardians, "He likes throwing antique rugs on fitted carpets, and the walls are so dense with art treasures that you barely see their surfaces. At one time, he even owned the house where Jane Austen had been raised." These characteristics would seem to situate him squarely in the Bertie Wooster mold.

Yet, beyond these predilections, the client seems more at home with the modern notion of the English gentleman. The townhouse exhibits a mix of art and possessions that is worldly and hip, which gives it a currency that makes it nothing if not contemporary. "His tastes are very cosmopolitan and he is apt to embrace a cross-pollination of cultures," explains Bradfield. "He's truly international."

Bradfield's client took this townhouse as a temporary abode while the designer completes a larger limestone residence for him. By no means small, it feels far greater than its square footage thanks to a series of grand illusions that Bradfield conjures up like a magician. The first of these is the trans-epochal vignette that greets visitors just to the left of the entry, where a pair of fine 18th-century English chairs juxtaposed with an antique rug stand before a gargantuan color photograph by Candida Hofer. The image depicts a long corridor of the Musée du Louvre.

OPENING PAGES: In the entrance hall Candida Hofer's overscaled "Musée du Louvre" photo conjures the feeling of an additional passage. Dylan Lewis's "Cheetah Head II" in the foreground.

LEFT: A detail of one of two exquisite Chinese cloisonné vases in the bedroom.

The scale is so immense that the viewer feels as if he or she could cross through the picture plane to stroll along the Louvre's parquet floors under an ornate vaulted ceiling and admire the murals overhead or the gilded Rococo moldings and boiserie along its walls. "It gives you a virtual corridor into an entirely different wing," says Bradfield.

One of the client's requests, observes Bradfield's associate Roric Tobin, was that "he wanted the 16-foot ceilings of the drawing room in his bedroom." This was physically impossible, of course. So, the team came up with an eccentric solution straight from the pages of *Brideshead Revisited*, a novel densely populated by the old manner of English gentlemen. Like Lord Marchmain in that book, who had his four-poster bed reconstructed in the Chinese drawing room of the castle, Bradfield and Tobin walled off their client's drawing room and converted it into a luxurious master suite. Again, its regal scale creates the illusion of something much grander.

The client also favored a four-poster bed, "not something we usually use," says Tobin. The end result was a highly customized version of an existing bed, which the design team altered to look more cleanly modern. (They had the footboard removed, created ruching that was simpler than the original design and detailed the posts with white gold collars).

Bradfield cunningly concealed the radiators with a window banquette where his client often finds quiet solace with a good book. The Oriental carpet and a pair of exquisite antique Chinese cloisonné vessels internationalize the setting. Contemporary Chinese art by Wei Rong gives the room a more provocative edge.

In her book, *The Image of the English Gentleman in Twentieth-Century Literature*, Christine Berberich asks Sir Sydney Waterloo, "one of the most perfect gentlemen of contemporary England," to define this persona in the context of today's world, to which Waterloo responds, "The gentleman is he who feels at ease in the presence of everyone and everything, and who makes everyone and everything feel at ease in his presence." The environment Bradfield has created for this client paves the way for this English gentleman to employ exactly that brand of grace.

RIGHT: A customized four-poster bed in the master bedroom is surrounded by Chinese art, including "Empress Dowager Enjoys the Opera #3" (top left) by Wei Rong.

"Great art picks up where nature ends."

—*Marc Chagall*

The London drawing room owned by Pauline de Rothschild and her husband, the poet-vintner Baron Philippe de Rothschild, was inspired by their trip to Communist Russia one frigid winter in the 1960s. It mixed contemporary and antique furnishings against a symphony of blues and grays: marbelized turquoise pilasters and entablatures, silvery gray Mongolian goatskin rugs, a custom steel sofa, gilt Louis XVI furniture upholstered in sky blue and oyster-colored taffeta. The curtains, an abundance of more silk taffeta, were cut at least a yard longer than necessary so they would puddle voluminously on the floor.

That unforgettable room is long gone, of course. But, were the Baronne alive today, she could stroll into the drawing room of this meandering 18,000-square-foot Hudson River estate designed by Bradfield and feel completely at home. Though not filled with Louis furniture, it shares a similar color scheme, an awe-inspiring sense of grandeur, a comparable mixture of custom furnishings and fine antiques, and those voluptuously puddled silk taffeta curtains. In fact, the startling congruities do not end there.

OPENING PAGES: The breathtaking entryway sports an 18-foot mirrored cabinet (left) at the base of a 24-foot-high mirrored wall, Ruhlmannesque sconces and a Botero sculpture. The railing Bradfield designed (right) was inspired by Art Moderne metalwork.

ABOVE: The living room's cool ice blue palette is a serene counterpoint to bold art by Sophia Vari, whose "Plenitude de l'Air" is visible in the hall, and Jim Dine's "Double Venus" in the foreground. Julie Hedrick's sublime "Snow, Sky and Thunder" canvas is above the sofa.

Pauline de Rothschild was a beauty with a keen mind, a tastemaker tremendously influential in the fields of fashion and interior design who also hosted a literary salon that fostered the talents of Yukio Mishima and Isak Dinesen. Bradfield's clients are people with a like sense of panache. "They're heavenly—young, and sophisticated. Like all cultivated Europeans, they speak several languages fluently. I looked to the great salons of the pre-war years for the design and Rothschild's London residence in Albany immediately sprung to mind."

The first impression one receives upon crossing the threshold is intoxicating—a double volume foyer with 24-foot ceilings, the walls lined in pale gray silk, "is multiplied over and over again," says Bradfield, "by a wall of mirror panels framed by classical pilasters." At the foot of this reflective surface, which boasts spectacular Ruhlmannesque sconces, is a custom low cabinet clad in antique mirror and measuring 18 feet in length. A bronze Botero nude dances jubilantly atop the cabinet, as if so elated by the space that she feels compelled to perform an arabesque à demi hauteur. It is impossible that, were they alive today, any member of Pauline de Rothschild's circle—designer Elsa Schiaparelli, director and lover John Huston, *Vogue* editor Diana Vreeland—would fail to be enthralled.

"I was intimately involved with the architecture," explains Bradfield, who worked with John Ike of Ike Kligerman Barkley Architects. "We reconfigured the rooms to create an open plan that flowed easily from the entry hall to the drawing room to a more intimate elevated area with a recessed bar. It's very gracious and palatial."

And, indeed, the spaces create an instinctive directional movement that carries the eye effortlessly along. It is a movement, both physical and visual, that is often aided by strategically curated and placed works of art. After the Botero sculpture, the next artwork one encounters is Sophia Vari's "Plenitude de l'Aire." Vari has said, "My intent is to take geometry, volume and shapes and humanize them in space." Like Botero's subject, the components of this deep blue construction seem to cavort in midair, cheerfully unbound by gravity. The two sculptures, though executed in completely different idioms, complement each other perfectly. Botero and Vari, who are husband and wife, seem to be working in marital tandem to draw visitors down the hall into the drawing room.

LEFT: Glass window walls draped in silk taffeta overlook a verdant landscape. Bradfield repeated the cord and vine pattern of the fabric as a border for the entrance staircase rug.

Upon arrival, one is immediately drawn to Jim Dine's "Double Venus" sculpture, its stance and form looking like nothing so much as the human incarnation of Vari's cubic shapes. The enormous room's Art Moderne furnishings, monochromatic color scheme and plush textures recall the salons of Coco Chanel, Yves Saint-Laurent and other Parisian couturiers of yesteryear. Bradfield has also subconsciously prepared guests for this room by referencing the intertwined cord and vine pattern of the armchairs' fabric in the border of the foyer's custom staircase rug. So, the act of entering this room is accompanied by a certain ineffable sense of comfort and familiarity. The quietude of the color scheme, combined with a contemplative canvas by Julie Hedrick (a Hudson Valley painter known for her atmospheric abstractions) and the sylvan setting visible through floor-to-ceiling walls of glass that ring the room, produce an instantaneous calm. "It's about serenity, but serenity with a very couture flair," says Bradfield.

LEFT: A custom Art Moderne wool and silk rug underlies sophisticated furnishings. On a coffee table at right is Joan Miró's bronze "Oiseau Migrateur Posé sur la Tête d'une Femme en Pleine Nuit."

In a departure from the amazing Rothschild parallels, Bradfield created a much more glamorous dining room than Pauline's in The Albany, which was, by all accounts, austere and conventional. That dining room had bare windows and rush mats on the floor (though the wall color had a chic derivation: it was said to have been copied from the effect of light passing through an Hermès umbrella). There is nothing austere or conventional in this dining room, however, which is appointed with a 1940s Venetian églomisé mirror and a quartet of sconces and a chandelier by Baccarat. There is also a slender Italian Art Deco buffet and exceptional modern art, such as Boschi's surrealistic abstracted male and female figures of bronze that occupy the center of attention on the table.

The effect of the master bedroom is that of the most well-dressed tree house imaginable. Directly above the drawing room, it is surrounded by the same leafy panorama, but its height makes it appear as if one is literally in the canopy of the forest. The channeled bed is upholstered in supple leather, like that used, says Bradfield, "on an Hermès bag." The custom silk rug, as well as the cut velvet fabric on a chaise that inspired it, bring a cultivated sense of nature into the room. And, when Bradfield's clients want to be hidden even from the surrounding woods, they can draw lush ivory silk taffeta curtains lined in pale lavender.

It would be the perfect place for the trendsetting Baronne to recline while reading Proust's *Remembrance of Things Past*, as she was known to do at three o'clock in the morning. In a *New York Times* article some years ago, the design writer Mitchell Owens, who was hard at work on a biography of Pauline, wrote, "What she read, whom she loved and where she traveled have been largely forgotten...but, how she lived is still part of the vocabulary of stylish living." It is a vocabulary that Bradfield has deployed here with great fluency.

LEFT: A Venetian eglomisé mirror in the dining room reflects a table set with Italian abstracted male and female forms executed in bronze by artist Valeria Boschi.

FOLLOWING PAGES: The master suite features pearlized acrylic "Bird of Paradise" lamps by Rougier on either side of a channeled bed. The silk custom carpet design is derived from a field of stylized Art Deco roses.

"*Every good artist creates what he is.*"

—*Jackson Pollack*

182

Dick Cooper, a retired investor and inveterate art collector, remembers the moment he saw Frank Stella's monumental construction "Midnight Forecastle" at a gallery briefly co-owned by Larry Gagosian and Leo Castelli in the 1980s. "I almost fell to my knees at the glory and grandeur of the piece," he says. He bought the 14-by-20-foot work on the spot. Yet, it would be almost 20 years before he found the right setting for the work, an 8,500-square-foot penthouse in Chicago's Park Hyatt tower.

Cooper purchased the apartment before it was erected, working with the builder to extend the ceilings upward to 16 feet, and called Bradfield to design the interiors. His decision was hardly random. Jay Spectre and Bradfield had decorated other projects for the client and his wife—an earlier Chicago apartment, a home in Winnetka, Illinois, and another in Palm Beach.

"The entrance hall was created with the sole purpose of featuring the Stella," says Bradfield. "It is all about theater. And about art." What else was needed, reasoned the designer, but reflective marble floors and an elegantly stepped ceiling? (Some Poillerat-inspired, Bradfield-designed metal gates, cinnabar palace vases and two bronze doré drape-leg consoles by Rateau eventually joined the Stella). And, there's drama here aplenty. Cooper recalls a visit by a museum curator some years ago. As one set of three elevator doors that open onto the hall parted, "I could hear him gasp," recalls Cooper.

Bradfield designed a study around a Jean-Michel Basquiat painting. "I've always connected to art history and the artists who were extending the boundaries," says Cooper of the painting. He first encountered the artist in a Sunday *New York Times* article about a Basquiat exhibit at Mary Boone Gallery.

OPENING PAGES: A rendering of the entrance hall (left) shows the placement of an enormous Frank Stella sculpture (right) so large that it had to be hoisted by helicopter to the 66th floor.

THESE PAGES: The study (drawing, right) was designed around an enormous Jean-Michel Basquiat painting (left) from Mary Boone Gallery.

"Dick immediately hopped on a plane and flew to New York," remembers Bradfield. "When he got there, most of the show had been sold. He was irredeemably bitten."

Of the painting he acquired there, Cooper says, "I responded to the pose. It was a very commanding posture of a black man standing there saying 'Here I am.'" Working from the extraordinary presence of the painting, Bradfield gave it free reign in the study, swathing the walls in zebrawood and adding low-slung built-in bookcases, a Ruhlmann desk and a custom sofa and carpet. Basquiat's man now presides over the room and its splendorous views of Lake Michigan.

Bradfield made his mark throughout the entire penthouse in similar fashion, allowing artworks to provide the raison d'etre of his designs for the rooms they inhabit. Painting and sculpture from Cooper's foundation—by the likes of such artists as Julian Schnabel, Jeff Koons, Roy Lichtenstein, George Condo, Maurizio Cattelan, Brice Marden, Damien Hirst, Keith Haring and others—were then incorporated into the renderings "before a single wall went up," the designer says. In fact, it would not be inaccurate to say that the apartment actually grew around, and for, the art.

"One of the hallmarks of my collection," observes Cooper, "is that much of the work is monumental. This presented a challenge to Geoffrey," whom he refers to as "an interior artist." Bradfield, however, more than rose to the challenge. The proof is in the client's great regard for Bradfield's talent. "He is in his field," avers Cooper, "like Frank Lloyd Wright was in architecture, or Picasso in painting, or Thoreau in literature. His work is transcendental. He takes you into his world and you are engulfed by a different sensibility. It changes the way you see. I think of Geoffrey as a great artist."

THESE PAGES: One of the drawing rooms (rendered below) features, among others,
a Julian Schnabel broken-plate portrait of the client's wife, Lana.

"This period of blue monochromes was the product of my pursuit of the indefinable in painting."

—Yves Klein

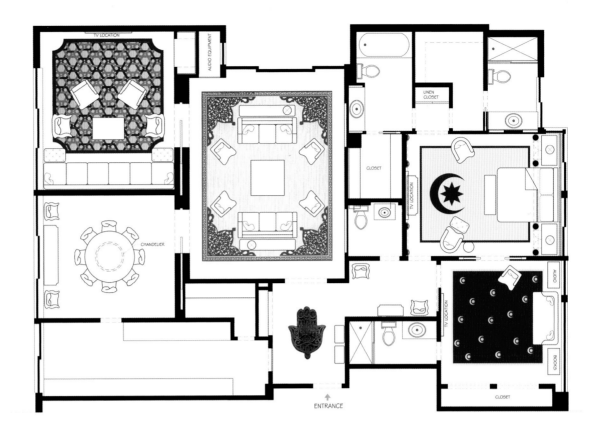

When Paul Bowles arrived in Morocco in 1931, he described its intoxicating exoticism in literally surrealistic terms: "If I said that Tangier struck me as a dream city, I should mean it in the strict sense…I relish the idea that in the night, all around me in my sleep, sorcery is burrowing its invisible tunnels in every direction…Spells are being cast…"

Like an alchemist extracting attar from rose petals, Bradfield has distilled that dreamy Maghrebian allure to its pure essence for this Palm Beach apartment. In a series of evocative rooms, he picks up the preferred blue-and-white palette of the clients and runs it through a mesmerizing gamut of fantasy. Most interestingly, his scheme illustrates how very few elements are required to create a modern tour de force.

The entire hypnotic composition is basically a masterful variation on four themes: the indigo-and-white color scheme, Moroccan fretwork, Moorish arches, and the reflection and refraction of light through the use of mirrors and acrylic furnishings. These elements are repeated again and again in various elegant guises throughout, cross-referencing each other from room to room, at once offering a unity of lush experience and lending an individual character to each space. "There was a tremendous amount of discipline and editing," says Bradfield…and it shows!

OPENING PAGES: A Moroccan pierced metal star curtain tie (left) gathers the drapery at the point where its ivory panel meets its blue skirting. An elegant enfilade through Moroccan arches (right) looking from the media room into the living room.

SECOND SPREAD: The foyer (left) with its custom Hand of Fatima rug and Luigi Benzoni's massive canvas reflected in the mirror. The pristine white living room (right) with Benzoni's counterpoint at center and (above) the apartment's floor plan.

THESE PAGES: A rendering of the living room (above) and the exceptional finished product (right), which looks out into a canopy of lush tropical palms.

Yet, the circumscribed palette and decorative vocabulary also gave Bradfield a delicious sort of freedom—the freedom of simplicity. Though the elements themselves, like the fretwork, may be ornate, the way they coalesce "is almost Zen-like," he says. Of course, this being a Bradfield project, it is a decidedly glamorous variety of Zen.

After the initial walk-through of the condominium residence with his clients, the vision of what it could be struck Bradfield so immediately and clearly that, he says, "I designed it on the flight back to New York. I sent them very, very preparatory sketches, and that is exactly how we proceeded with the design."

Moroccan style is actually not ill suited to the Palm Beach environment. Much of the Venetian interiors that are ubiquitous here already incorporate Moroccan elements. The bright sunlight is something else the two locales have in common and, believes the designer, "If ever a country demanded the use of white, it would be Morocco."

So Bradfield's design called for a series of immaculate white rooms separated by Moorish arches, some pointed horseshoe in form, others multifoil. "I wanted to take down bearing walls to create symmetry in those rooms," he says. Leslie Pearce of Palm Beach-based Smith Architectural Group "made it happen," recalls Bradfield. "They helped move the project along efficiently."

Practically every inch is custom, starting in the entrance hall, which sports a handmade rug in the shape of a *khamsa*, the North African talisman that depicts the hand of Fatima, the daughter of the prophet Mohammed. Bradfield juxtaposes this with an ineluctable painting called "Modulazione Blu" by Venetian contemporary painter and sculptor Luigi Benzoni. The artist is known for works that depict, in the words of his London gallery, Collier & Dobson, "an anxious and restless face of a man who seems to have lost the notion of his own being" (not unlike many a Bowles character, coincidentally). The contrast between the human and the holy here is subtly ravishing.

THESE PAGES: The media room rug picks up the pattern of the fretwork on the walls (left) and mixes custom furniture with handmade Moroccan tables. Fretwork pocket doors (right) in opened and closed positions.

The foyer leads to a living room that introduces the major themes. The corner element of the white custom rug is carved with a deep blue pattern derived from Moroccan tile design. Bradfield picks that motif up in the border of mirrored panels in the dining room. These panels are outlined in star-patterned Moorish tile, a theme repeated in turn in the outer border of the living room rug. By deploying this sort of cross-referencing, Bradfield unites the spaces without succumbing to a monotonous décor.

Other congruities abound. Another tile-derived pattern was embroidered onto the skirts of armchairs in the living room. ("Getting the embroidery accomplished was a feat," says Bradfield, noting that the fabric was a heavy cotton chenille). He carried it throughout the apartment by translating the pattern into custom ceiling moldings framing each space. It shows up again at the border of the mosaic tile work in the dining room. Four-inch-thick pocket doors separating the rooms sport fretwork patterns that recur in larger or smaller format throughout the house, namely on the media room rug, but, also wrapped around built-in bedside tables in the master chamber.

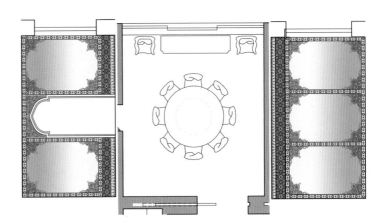

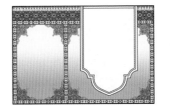

PREVIOUS PAGES: The mesmerizing mirrored dining room features a Murano chandelier suspended above Bradfield's "Medici" table and "Lady Mendl" chairs amidst an ornate Moorish mosaic, tile and fretwork fantasy.

BELOW: Bradfield unifies spaces by pulling patterns from the intricate border ornamentation (rendering right) for rug, molding and furniture designs throughout the rest of the apartment.

ABOVE: The blue mirror behind the master bed imparts a feeling of twilight.

FOLLOWING PAGES: Bradfield designed the wing chair and the rug (left). The drawings are by Peter Max. In the powder room (right) an Urban Archaeology sink is set against an ornamented mirrored horseshoe arch.

Finally, clear and reflective surfaces bounce and play with the abundant natural light in the various rooms. This task is left up to acrylic furniture in the living room, dining room and master bedroom, as well as strategically placed mirrors that fill some of the Moorish arches. The mirrors also serve to amplify the spaces: facing mirrored panels placed on exactly the same axis in the living and media rooms create the illusion of an enfilade of four rooms rather than two.

The media room is the only departure, albeit a barely perceptible one, from the indigo-and-white palette. Bradfield enjoys designing one room in a bold color so that, when the doors are open, it is like a surprise amongst the monochrome that identifies the rest of the spaces. This would not have worked in this apartment, as it would have confused the symmetry he devised with the mirrors. So in that room, he explains, "I felt strongly that it be more ivory." It is just enough to set the room—which, with its floor-to-ceiling leather-tufted banquette, showcases a more continental aesthetic—apart from the adjacent spaces.

The master bedroom is a complete sensory indulgence. Blue glass behind the headboard infuses the chamber with twilight glamour. An extravagant Dennis Basso chinchilla fur warms the bed. A custom carpet with a star and sickle moon is dramatically graphic and probably, along with the Fatima hand rug in the foyer, the most overtly North African reference. But, on the wall are silver-leaf frames exhibiting a collection of drawings by American artist Peter Max.

"Knowing how to free oneself is nothing," wrote André Gide, another dévotée of North Africa. "The difficulty is knowing how to live with that freedom." Bradfield illustrates commandingly that he knows precisely how.

"*Art is not what you see, but what you make others see.*"

—*Edgar Degas*

The world's royalty has made an art of the grand entrance, orchestrating slowly unfolding pageants of experience unapologetically calculated to elicit awe. It begins with the precise military detail, which is followed by heralds and drums, then carriages conveying courtiers, and finally reaching its crescendo, the monarch. It's all about building expectation and moment, and it has to be perfectly paced to ensure the desired response.

Bradfield understands this. "'The secret to being a bore is to tell everything,'" he says, quoting Voltaire. "You always hold something back." He follows this concept to its logical conclusion in his scheme for the penthouse apartment of a prominent Palm Beach hostess and her husband, his third collaboration with the couple. "What I was trying to achieve here is a sense of procession," he explains. "The space is designed for entertaining. My client is a celebrated hostess and very accomplished. There are those who really take up the social gauntlet and run with it." This lady is one of these.

OPENING PAGES: A detail of Joan Mitchell's "Dogs Only."

BELOW: An arresting Kenneth Noland target painting makes an intense impact before entering a second set of custom-designed bronze and gilt doors.

RIGHT: These lead into a gold-leafed domed space with a Lalique pendant lamp and a mosaic floor.

So, rather than a long, straight passage leading gracelessly to the main event—a drawing room with panoramic views of the intercoastal and ocean from its deep wraparound terrace, and a glimmering, silvery dining room—Bradfield composes a play in three acts, guiding his audience along an unhurried progression of anterooms, moving through prosceniums of custom Gilbert Poillerat-inspired bronze and gilt doors, each one unfolding onto a new and exciting visual tableau.

Emerging from the elevators through the first set of doors, which are glazed to allow light to infiltrate, guests come upon a breathtaking Kenneth Noland painting. "The artistry and discipline of Noland is extraordinary," says Bradfield. The work is the centerpiece of a composition that is modern, simple and taut. Stepping through the next door into an octagonal space reveals a mosaic floor set with semiprecious stones and illuminated by a 1930s Lalique ceiling pendant and two gilt Art Moderne sconces.

Advancing on, one passes a major Jean Dubuffet painting and entrances to a library and the dining room (the latter behind the third set of bronze and gilt doors), finally arriving at the drawing room. "It was quite a departure for me," says Bradfield of this room, "because it's far more conservative than what I am apt to do. But, the request was for something more traditional."

LEFT: The Mitchell painting and Lipschitz's reclining nude sculpture are contemporary notes in a predominantly traditional drawing room.

BELOW: The penthouse's living room has French doors that lead out to impressive wraparound terraces with views of the intercoastal. Bradfield created symmetry in this oddly shaped space with separate seating areas anchored by a roundabout.

To be sure, the presence of a floral print on two armchairs is not exactly expected from this designer. However, many other Bradfield hallmarks are immediately apparent: the custom Bradfield-designed rug, the sumptuous curtains that puddle on the floor beneath the French doors...the mix of periods.

Regrettably, there were also two monumental supporting columns in this space that Bradfield had to contend with, as well as angles that were skewed and odd. "Even asymmetrical compositions, ideally, should achieve symmetry," believes Bradfield, so he devised seating areas at either end of the room and anchored them with a large borne at the center. Drawing from the owners' extensive modern art collection, he faced off Joan Mitchell's "Dogs Only" and "Violett," a Gerhard Richter canvas, their very different colors and abstractions (one is primarily orange, the other silvery gray and magenta; one artist's brushstrokes are vertical, the other's horizontal) carrying on a lively visual discourse across the room.

THESE PAGES: Three eras come together (below) in this grouping of a French bombé chest, a Japanese bronze vessel and an 18th-century bérgère. The Richter painting (right) and a Tang Dynasty horse define another seating area.

The original open-plan footprint of the 7,000-square-foot apartment lacked a separate dining room, clearly an indispensable space for Bradfield's client. So, the designer carved one from the drawing room, then made it eminently adaptable to various sorts of gatherings by introducing three tables rather than one, which can be combined when necessary. "This gal is glamorous," says Bradfield by way of explaining the custom silver Gracie wallpaper that surrounds the room. "It was her request to use the Chinese wallpaper. We had Gracie take out many of the elements to simplify it" (Bradfield ardently believes Isaac Newton's observation that "Truth is ever to be found in the simplicity, and not in the multiplicity, of things").

LEFT: A view of the dining room through Gilbert Poillerat-inspired bronze and gilded doors. Two crystal and gilt sconces illuminate the Art Moderne sideboard.

BELOW: By introducing three tables, the dining room was made more adaptable for entertaining. The clock is 18th-century French. Bradfield modernized the Gracie traditional wallpaper by editing and eliminating elements, simplifying the pattern.

"Even asymmetrical compositions, ideally, should achieve symmetry."

—*Geoffrey Bradfield*

Across the hall is the library. "I designed this room around the Pousette-Dart painting on the south wall," explains Bradfield. "Although we wanted the library to have a masculine feel, we also wanted to retain a feeling of light." So, rather than opt for the entire paneled effect, Bradfield had the room configured with wood moldings and paneled from the floor up to chair-rail height. Then, he expressed the remaining vertical space with beige raffia and had the ceiling stenciled in bamboo.

The hues of "Imploding White," the Pousette-Dart painting, and Theodoros Stamos's "Red Field" on an adjacent wall determined the color palette. Red dominates here, appearing on the Bradfield-designed rug, the upholstery of two armchairs, the embossed leather of a bérgère and desk chair. The color offers a bold backdrop for elegant antiques, including a substantial Empire gilt and alabaster chandelier and a 19th-century game table.

By the time visitors have retired to the library, Bradfield and his client have achieved their desired impression: luxury as the expression of beauty. They leave with the same sense of ceremony through the graceful procession of anterooms and doors, feeling a bit like participants in a royal cortège themselves.

RIGHT: A major Dubuffet painting in the hall is visible from the library. Bradfield designed the loop and heavily cut-pile carpet.

FOLLOWING PAGES: The library draws its color scheme from Pousette-Dart's "Imploding White" (left) and Theodoros Stamos's "Red Field." Bradfield avoided a heavy feeling by mixing the rich paneling with surfaces of raffia.

LEFT: This anteroom, dominated by an oversized Eric Fischl flesh-toned nude painting and sparsely furnished with Neapolitan tabourets and a gilt mirror, leads to the master suite.

ABOVE: The client requested period furnishings and a romantic mood for the master bedroom. Sumptuous window treatments featuring balloon shades of rose colored silk taffeta frame water views of the famous Biltmore. A silver *maquette* sculpture by Arnaldo Pomodoro sits on the night table.

"*Taste is the only morality!*"

—*John Ruskin*

The Mediterranean proclivities of the Palm Beach set are well-established. The ocean and intercoastal are fronted with countless Mizner- and Fatio-inspired Spanish casitas and Venetian-style palazzos. There are those few idiosyncratic personalities who have strayed from that norm—notably in the past Marjorie Merriweather Post, who commissioned Joseph Urban to design several Deco-inspired rooms at Mar-a-Lago (including the bedroom suite of her daughter, the actress Dina Merrill).

An adventuresome client of Bradfield's, investor George Mann, recently moved from one of these Fatio mansions, acquiring a 5,000-square-foot house designed in the Art Deco style. He hired Bradfield, well known for his contemporary interpretations of this distinctive era, to address the stark interiors.

"Architecturally, it was a very cube-like form from the outside, with a U-shape interior embracing an enclosed courtyard and pool." Much to his chagrin, an existing spiraled staircase rose clumsily from the center of the drawing room to the upper floor, "making it impossible to arrange furniture." It was, Bradfield says, as unsightly and absurd as "a waxed military moustache."

The designer had the stair removed, replacing it with a brushed tubular steel and Macassar ebony version along a far wall that looks straight out of a 1930s RKO musical. "You can see Fred Astaire and Ginger Rogers coming down those stairs," says Bradfield. "It lost none of our theatrical intent." In fact, the home leans more toward the Donald Desky genre of urbanity. The initial inspiration for the drawing room rug he designed, for instance, was a Jacques-Emile Ruhlmann textile. Its Jazz Age marquee-like imagery also recalls the dazzling décor of Radio City Music Hall and the Roxy apartment, or the electric zigzag patterns on a backdrop for a Busby Berkeley number.

Bradfield gave glamour an additional nudge, designing many of the Macassar ebony furnishings based on Ruhlmann originals, including a bed with a veneered sunburst headboard worthy of a pajama-clad Clark Gable. Mirrored walls, lush fabrics (ivory silk curtains lined with scarlet taffeta in the drawing room, copper taffeta in the library) and high-polish surfaces in every room amplify shimmer and shine, particularly in the evening, broadcasting an irresistibly suave sophistication.

OPENING PAGES: A monumental Enrique Mancini head was lowered by crane alongside the pool and boxed on three sides with black mirror.

PREVIOUS PAGES: The view of the drawing room from the fireplace directly opposite the Mancini head. Bradfield's design for the custom rug evokes the Jazz Age.

TOP: Bradfield removed a circular staircase from the center of the room, replacing it with a sleeker and less obtrusive steel version along one wall. A group of bronze minstrels by Lambert-Rucki is at the foot of the stair.

LEFT: A black Louise Nevelson wall sculpture contrasts the red lacquered piano. The fire screen is by Edgar Brandt.

The custom furniture was made in France to Bradfield's exacting specifications, and the level of craftsmanship ensures they hold their own against important antiques purchased abroad, such as signed Gilbert Poillerat consoles in the entry and an Edgar Brandt fire screen. "I searched for Art Deco items on my own in Paris," says Mann, "but I was confronted by such variety that I became confused. Geoffrey and I made the second trip together and because of his expertise he was able to organize the whole spree in 24 hours!"

But, glamour can appear skin deep unless its underpinnings have a degree of seriousness. Here, that gravity emanates from museum-quality art, much of it with a Surrealist aura. The 1920s and '30s, of course, were the movement's acme, and much of the home's art—whether literally from the period or not—reflects the dark, dreamlike states the Surrealists were fond of depicting.

None of the artworks conveys this more so than the presence of a monumental Enrique Mancini head sculpture that gazes into the living room from across the courtyard pool. A contemporary piece, its weight is so stupendous that it had to be lowered into place with the use of a crane. Landscape designer Mario Nievera planted lush tropical foliage that seems to sprout from the head. The white marble mass appears to float above a black pool, an illusion Bradfield accomplished by boxing it in with black mirror. The head is colossal, powerful and, while undeniably beautiful, also enigmatically challenging.

RIGHT: Ivory silk curtains lined in scarlet taffeta. In the corner of the drawing room, a Macassar ebony French commode supports a bronze sculpture by Dupagne.

*"Glamour is the power to
rearrange people's emotions."*
— *Arthur Miller*

LEFT: Albert Gleizes's "Composition à Deux Personages" and a painting by R. Renneson bring a Surrealist edge to luxurious furnishings and appointments in the library, including copper taffeta curtains and striped burlap walls.

ABOVE: Bradfield accentuated the chagrin diamond pattern on the wall with polished steel nailheads. A metal relief by Roy Lichtenstein seems to float on a mirrored wall. This exceptional art collection is the result of a collaboration with Palm Beach art dealer Arij Gasiunasen.

A series of doors was eliminated in the drawing room, opening it up to the courtyard with a wall of glass, establishing a dialogue between the head and the room's Macassar ebony and brushed steel mantel. "The drawing room and the courtyard become one; two points of visual reference being the fireplace and the Mancini head," says Bradfield. "They're exactly opposite each other, totally aligned. One is in, one is out, and there's a definitive synergy between the interior and exterior."

The Mancini seems to corroborate the Belgian Surrealist painter Paul Delvaux's observation: "What is Surrealism? In my opinion, it is above all the reawakening of the poetic idea in art, the reintroduction of the subject, but in a very particular sense, that of the strange and illogical." Bradfield's use of this sculpture balances its incongruity of scale with the poetry of ordered symmetry.

There's a tantalizing and imposing illogic to the presence of a Louise Nevelson construction above the drawing room piano too; one has the sense of easily disappearing into the depths of its inky blackness. Similarly, an R. Renneson painting in the library is superficially decorative, but the subject matter also conveys an undercurrent of torrid sensuality, as if the viewer has entered a vaguely predatory Garden of Eden. In the same room, Albert Gleizes's 1921 "Composition à Deux Personages" is of the period, but it peddles an angular, abstracted Cubism rather than the attenuated sentimentality of, say, Erté. In the bedroom, a Roberto Matta canvas is frankly and undeniably Surrealist.

Interestingly, the contrast serves to heighten the glamour of the furnishings and materials. "Glamour," said the playwright Arthur Miller, "is the power to rearrange people's emotions." Certainly Bradfield has achieved that. And, he did it without resorting to the ubiquitous Mediterranean predictability that reigns in Palm Beach.

PREVIOUS PAGES: The master bedroom's aqua striae walls are drawn from the oceanic shades of the Matta painting. A masculine radiused headboard was custom made of Macassar ebony.

RIGHT: "Femme Nu aux Bras Levés," a sculpture by Joseph Csaky, strikes an alluring pose on a Ruhlmann-inspired chest that Bradfield had fabricated in France.

"*Above all, it is a matter of loving art, not understanding it.*"

—Fernand Léger

OPENING PAGES: "Les Trois Soeurs" by Fernand Léger is one work in the extensive collection of 20th-century masters the clients have amassed over the years.

ABOVE: Larry Rivers's "Two Women" and, beyond the sliding glass doors, a pair of Lalanne sheep surveying the pounding surf.

RIGHT: An amalgam of fine contemporary art comprising Milton Avery, Roy Lichtenstein, Niki de Saint-Phalle, Pablo Picasso, Alexander Calder, Diego Giacometti and David Hockney harmonize in this drawing room overlooking the ocean.

For over a century, the parade of Vanderbilts, Astors, Carnegies and Morgans who made their way to Palm Beach came primarily for the weather and the spectacular ocean views. And there has never been a better perspective from which to take in those views than The Breakers, the Schultz & Weaver-designed resort built by Henry Flagler. Any apartment here must concede to the ocean as its focal point...or should it?

When a residence is, as Bradfield describes, "the most important penthouse in Palm Beach," a designer can be forgiven for daring to challenge the supremacy of that view by exercising some decorative muscle of his own. "Every piece is truly refined and precious," says Bradfield of the art, objects and accessories he assembled here. From the gilded caryatids of the dining room's buffet to its ornate gilt and ebonized Gustavian chairs, this sprawling abode is a jewel box of earthly treasures.

Major collectors, the couple who own this Breakers residence wanted it to be a showcase for their art. Bradfield was more than happy to oblige, juxtaposing great works of modern art by Fernand Léger, Fernando Botero, Larry Rivers and others with unparalleled 18th- and 19th-century European antiques and Tang Dynasty ceramics. Add to this amalgam a touch of whimsy: the Niki de Saint-Phalle trio of frolicking bathers and a pair of Lalanne sheep meadowed on a balcony overlooking the sea.

"It has been my privilege to work for these wonderful people for over 30 years," says Bradfield, sincerely. "The wife and I share a particular level of taste. We literally finish each others sentences." Relationships of such longevity tend to breed a finely tuned understanding between decorator and client that is rare today. It tends equally to breed an editing process that is as sharp as a surgeon's scalpel.

Every gesture here is confident and mature. There is not one superfluous element. And, against the backdrop of the Palm Beach surf, the sense of society and formality that made The Breakers such a legendary destination for royalty, aristocracy and celebrity reigns supreme. Bradfield has created something that draws on the Gilded Age opulence, that established this resort as world famous, but also brings it strikingly and irrevocably into the present.

RIGHT: The mix of eras in the dining room is one of intrigue: a Tang Dynasty camel, Gustavian chairs and 20th-century art by Léger and Fernando Botero (reflected in the mirror).

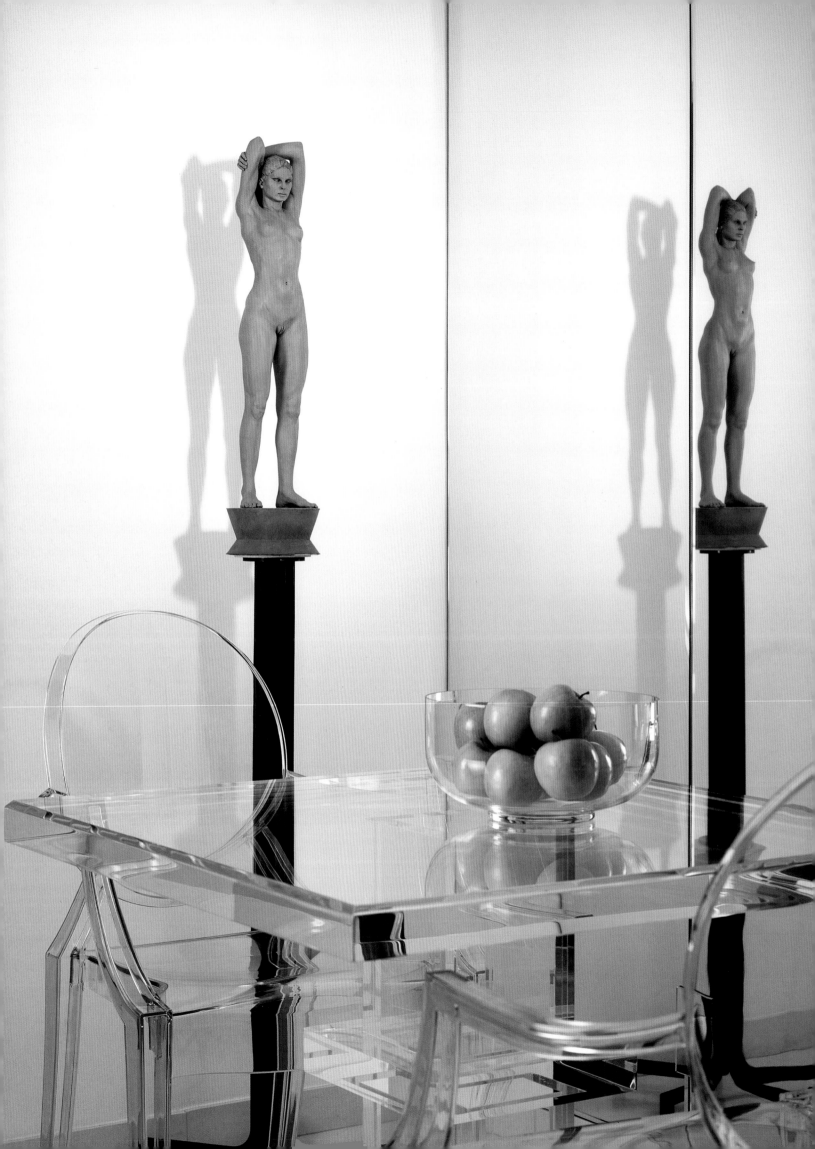

"*The exact limitations of one's taste should be an intense pleasure.*"

—*The Hon. Stephen Tennant*

When Stephen Tennant, the most decadent of England's "Bright Young Things," arrived in New York on the Berengaria, his friend David Herbert received him at the gangway. Herbert recalled watching Tennant disembark, "Marcelled and painted, delicately holding a spray of cattleya orchids." The customs official, appalled at Tennant's flamboyance, gruffly told him he should pin the flowers on, to which Tennant replied, "Oh, have you got a pin—you kind, kind creature?"

Bradfield's rapturous Palm Beach apartment captures the spirit of Tennant's scandalous insouciance, as well as what Tennant described as his own "fatal gift of beauty." It is unapologetically sensual and glamorous, and it delights in its own image, which is infinitely reflected in mirrored walls that, says Bradfield, "indulge make-believe."

The main room completely flouts convention of any kind, gleefully commingling classicism, Art Moderne, African primitivism and contemporary art. Four fluted Doric columns support an elegantly stepped ceiling, which hovers over a sisal rug Bradfield had painted in a 1940s-style pattern. He framed facing mirrored walls with Art Moderne-shaped moldings, which creates the illusion that the room's fabulousness grows exponentially as it repeats itself infinitely into space. The room is filled with intriguing textural juxtapositions: the sisal against the ivory Ultrasuede of the custom sofas, Cameroon fertility figures covered in cowrie shells against the immaculate white lacquer bookshelves they sit on, a thickly impastoed Julie Hedrick canvas against the perfect reflective smoothness of mirror.

OPENING PAGES: Robert Graham's seductive "Gabrielle" sculpture overlooks a "Shogun" table from Bradfield's Millennium Modern collection.

PREVIOUS PAGES: The living room juxtaposes diverse textures, transparent and mirrored surfaces that play with light and a rug handpainted with an Art Moderne motif.

RIGHT: Cowrie shell-clad fertility figures from Cameroon stand on a white lacquer cabinet, facing a 1940s silver crab sculpture.

Off the dining area—itself so transparent, with its acrylic furniture and mirrored wall, that it feels as if it's almost not there—is an alcove that serves as media room and bar. "I enveloped the diminutive space," explains Bradfield, "by having an artist execute a lush tropical cage of massive green leaves on both the walls and the ceiling." The room is a fecund tropicalia shot through with the chic sophistication of a floor-to-ceiling white leather tufted banquette (itself and two matching ottomans extravagantly fringed in wide white flax passementerie). The irresistible implication of this cage? Bradfield, a consummate aesthete in the wilds of the jungle.

"Color is so affecting," says Bradfield of the media room's high spirits. The explosion of green would have unhinged the hypersensitive Tennant, who once, while discussing favorite colors with a friend, exclaimed, "Oh, pink! I almost faint when I think of pink." It is an anecdote Bradfield clearly appreciates and relishes.

The designer's wittiest gestures, however, are reserved for the master bedroom. Art is always a vital, integral element of Bradfield's designs. But, usually its function is to impart a kind of impressive blue-chip heft to the rooms it inhabits. Here, however, the art—while unquestionably important—seems to inject equal parts joy and naughtiness. Jim Dine's "Heart" is pure jubilation rendered in Technicolor. Two Bradfield portraits by Hunt Slonem playfully juggle orange, red, pink, green and blue circles around the designer's handsome features. And, a witty exchange transpires across the bed between two sculptures: Sabin Howard's "Anger" and Edwina Sandys's "Eve's Apple." Bradfield teasingly acknowledges that fury combined with temptation can be a heady aphrodisiac.

Yet, there is sincere affection here too. Beside the bed is a modern chartreuse Eclipse chair. "It's the signature piece of Jay Spectre's and my furniture collection," explains Bradfield. "I've always kept one. It's like a good luck charm."

TOP: Stylized 1940s framed mirrors, classical columns and a stepped ceiling add architectural interest to the living room space.

LEFT: Custom upholstered furnishings in ivory Ultrasuede are raised on brushed steel feet, affording a comfortable view of the tropical vista outside. The "Clear Conscience" coffee table is from Bradfield's Millennium Modern collection.

"It's totally obvious to me that Geoffrey Bradfield designs environments in layers, making a syntax where a sculpture or painting will be the object or the focal point of the whole enterprise."

—*Julian Schnabel*

BELOW: The media room is in an alcove off the dining area, offering an exuberance of lush color to an otherwise white space.

RIGHT: Bradfield had an artist hand-paint the walls with jungle foliage and hung Sally Michel Avery's brightly colored "Pink Shirt" on a mirrored wall. The floor-to-ceiling tufted banquette faces a flat-screen TV.

BELOW: Bradfield matched the shape of the headboard to the 1940s-style framed mirrored panels in the living room.

RIGHT: The artist Hunt Slonem painted two portraits of Bradfield. This example hangs on the mirror opposite the bed.

Bradfield has compared the feel of this apartment to the film sets of *All About Eve*. But, while in that film Eve Harrington (played by an amoral conniving Anne Baxter) steals the limelight from Margo Channing (an acid-tongued Bette Davis), there is no one here to rob the designer of his stardom. This apartment is "All About Bradfield," in the most exuberant sense of the phrase.

LEFT: Jim Dine's Technicolor "Heart" from the Gasiunasen Gallery and a chair from Bradfield and Spectre's Signature collection add brilliant energy to the scene. Sabin Howard's "Anger" is on the other side table.

ABOVE: Edwina Sandys's temptation, "Eve's Apple," is on one of a pair of silver gueridon bedside tables.

*"I express myself in sculpture
since I am not a poet."*

—Aristide Maillol

"Every child is an artist. The challenge is remaining an artist when we grow up."

—*Pablo Picasso*

Appearances, the saying goes, can be deceiving. A look at the exterior of this palatial mansion on Palm Beach's exclusive Clarke Avenue—with its terra cotta tile roof and ivy-clad stucco walls—one could easily deduce that a dark and heavy Spanish extravaganza lies just inside the threshold. Instead, what greets visitors is a pristine interior of pastels and modern gallery-like settings. Bradfield describes the rotunda, which houses the grand stairway, as "an almost Le Corbusier-like space." The spirit of it, he explains, is not unlike the Villa Savoye in Poissy, arguably the most famous structure ever to come off the drawing boards of this father of International Style.

"Home life today is being paralyzed by the deplorable notion that we must have furniture," wrote Le Corbusier, née Charles Édouard Jeanneret-Gris, to Madame Savoye when she had the temerity to request that a chair and two sofas be added to the living room plan. And, indeed, Bradfield's design for the rotunda is artfully spare. The sole object here is a deliciously surreal sculpture of an apple, a monkey perched on its stem, by Claude and François-Xavier Lalanne. The ascent to the second floor, via a graceful spiral staircase, is lit only by a large lantern and two pairs of Diego Giacometti sconces. That is perfectly "It."

"Our desire was for something clean and pared down, something fresh and sophisticated and not the expected Spanish interiors," says Bradfield. So he took a couture turn with the Lalanne (the sculptor duo were the darlings of the 1960s haute set, counting Chanel, Valentino and Saint Laurent among their avid collectors). It is a cleverly succinct way to signal that the English knight and his lady who live here are discerning collectors, more modern in their tastes than many denizens of this gilded Treasure Coast island.

White and pale beige tones create a clean, yet warm, backdrop for a number of thoughtfully conceived and judiciously applied details. Bradfield does not ignore all reference to locale. However, his allusions are superbly subtle. A Murano glass chandelier in the dining room suggests a Venetian theme that is commonly taken over the top in Palm Beach. Spain is also represented, but by a collection of Pablo Picasso ceramics, rather than majolica or austere, tapestry furniture.

The ceramics, produced under Picasso's supervision from 1947 to 1971 at the Madoura Pottery in Vallauris, France, exude a rustic countenance and folkloric imagery that identifies them as quintessentially Iberian, bringing an unaffected contrast to more elegant materials like marble and etched glass. In 1999, when a selection of these was exhibited at the Metropolitan Museum of Art in New York, the critic Roberta Smith described them in a manner that captures the ambience of this entire residence: "Perhaps the *naive* status traditionally accorded ceramics had a relaxing effect [on Picasso]," she wrote, "contributing to the air of 'genius on holiday.'"

Genius is certainly stripped to its bare essentials here. And, these elegantly minimalist volumes give it ample room to run free.

PREVIOUS PAGES: The Mediterranean ivy-covered exterior offers little hint of the modern minimalist sophistication within. The tower (left) is just off the foyer and houses a gracefully curving stairway and Lalanne sculpture (right), illuminated by a lantern and two pairs of sconces, both by Diego Giacometti.

LEFT: Lalanne's whimsical, slightly surreal bronze sculpture of an apple with a monkey on its stem anchors the stairwell rotunda.

LEFT: Custom wrought iron gates lead to a modern dining room rich in details—including Art Deco-patterned wallpaper and a carved glass table beneath a Murano glass chandelier from the 1940s.

ABOVE: The dining room table is set with Jean Cocteau china and pieces of the owners' extensive collection of Picasso ceramics.

"*I was drawn to water intuitively, with a camera in my hand…drawn to its pulsing waves and undulating surfaces, and optically to the images it reflected.*"

—*Bill Viola*

OPENING PAGES: An Art Deco hammered silvered metal mirror in the foyer.

ABOVE: An oversized sculptural still life by Fernando Botero faces an Edgar Brandt console through custom gates in the entrance hall.

For centuries the sea has been an infinite and spellbinding source of inspiration for artists of every stripe: from Homer to Melville, Turner's impressionistic maritime paintings to Hugh Lane's harborscapes, Ashton's *Ondine* to Debussy's *La Mer*. And it is the sea—in this case the azure waters of Biscayne Bay and the Atlantic beyond—that informs the interiors of the winter home Bradfield designed for a prominent art-collecting couple from Ohio (see *An American Chateau*, page 52, which showcases their more landlocked Midwest residence).

The impressive 8,000-square-foot aerie, with wraparound terraces floating on the top floor of the Ritz-Carlton Residences, hovers above sweeping coastal views. "It's like a yacht with no boundaries," Bradfield says of the apartment.

The designer's scheme embraces the imagery of his summers off Sardinia and Capri. "It is a world where stupendous wealth congregates on these floating palaces...not unlike a royal armada." Returning to one's boat on a tender after a night of on-shore carousing, he explains, "All the hulls are lit up from beneath, which seems to illuminate the entire ocean floor. It makes the yachts appear to be floating on glass."

Another successful collaboration with West Coast architect Don Goldstein resulted in the rooms being superbly reconfigured, achieving a more open plan that afforded expansive vistas, emphasizing the maritime perspective. Bradfield drew inspiration for the décor from those views, sometimes quite literally, as evidenced by the living room rug, designed to resemble whitecaps on a restless sea. That is exactly the effect, complete with the sense of windswept forward motion on display outside the windows on any breezy day.

The sensation of movement continues on the wall, with a painting commissioned from James Nares, a British artist whose technique is to acrobatically suspend himself above the canvas and paint with huge calligraphy brushes he makes by hand. In language that uncannily befits the oceanside surroundings, art critic Donald Kuspit once described Nares's paintings this way: "The sense of constantly making painterly waves, and churning them in oscillating centrifugal and centripetal action, calls to mind dramatic decorative calligraphy." Nares, he concluded, had single-handedly rescued action painting from becoming just "another outdated historical style." Here, it looks anything but passé.

PREVIOUS PAGES: Tom Otterness's sculpture "Mad Mama" at left and a monumental alabaster vase by Marguerite de Bayser-Gratry, circa 1920, are the only vertical appointments in a room that is kept low-slung to take advantage of the view.

ABOVE: The custom rug executed by Stark Carpet and calligraphic painting by British artist James Nares mimic the restless motion of the ocean beyond.

RIGHT: The view from the living room into the dining room, where a wall paneled in mirror repeats the marine vistas, giving the impression of being completely surrounded by water.

FOLLOWING PAGES: Dale Chihuly's "Sea Form" glass sculptures serve as the dramatic centerpiece on a Gilbert Poillerat table surrounded by 12 Ruhlmann carved mahogany and ivory chairs.

LEFT: A round iron Poillerat table in the media room with gilt accents. A Bradfield custom-designed rug deploys a more abstracted representation of waves.

BELOW: The bamboo leaf breakfast table was specially commissioned from François-Xavier Lalanne.

RIGHT: Vibrant yellow accents in the media room under a painting by Roy Lichtenstein.

"For the period furnishings, I referenced the glory days of the famed Normandie and the S.S. France."

—Geoffrey Bradfield

BELOW: A six-foot-wide corridor becomes a gallery for Andy Warhol's worthy portfolio, his tribute to "Famous Jews," including the Marx Brothers, Franz Kafka, Sigmund Freud and Gertrude Stein.

RIGHT: Bradfield had Chagall's celebrated painting, "La Baie des Anges" interpreted in mosaic tile on the powder room walls. The vanity is made from slabs of "cloudy" marble originally used by Philip Johnson for the sculpture garden of the Museum of Modern Art in New York and salvaged by Urban Archaeology.

For the period furnishings, Bradfield referenced the glory days of the famed Normandie and the S.S. France. "It was an amalgam of great talent that produced those enthralling interiors," says Bradfield, adding, "I used almost all Art Deco furniture." Much of it came through B. Steinitz in Paris, which had assembled many of the museum-quality antiques that fill the owners' Ohio home. Art Deco was not Steinitz's specialty—18th-century French being the firm's custom. But, Bradfield explains, "A sense of trust had been established previously with the clients regarding authenticity of acquisitions. I did not want to go to another dealer to accomplish these finds."

The antiquarians rose to the challenge. In the entry hall, within sight of a theatrically over-sized white still life sculpture by Fernando Botero, is an Edgar Brandt console, the first of many exquisite pieces from the era that lie within. The dining room table has a gilded and silvered wrought iron base by Gilbert Poillerat. The top had been marble, but because it was in ill repair (and possibly not original), Bradfield had it replaced with a two-and-a-half-inch-thick slab of beveled acrylic, "so, you could enjoy fully, Poillerat's artistry." He complemented the table with signed mahogany and ivory Ruhlmann chairs and juxtaposed the combination with a modern buffet of his own design, which he faced in ivory shagreen and suspended in midair off the mirrored wall.

Bradfield's unique approach respects both the casual nature of a vacationing beach culture and the glamour of the prestigious address. "For all the fantasy, these clients are the most unpretentious people," he says. "Beloved young grandchildren and two pet dogs have free reign. It's really about family and friends."

That meant comfort was also a priority. Thus, bespoke upholstered furnishings feature deep seats that encourage lounging. Such is the case with the navy sofa and butter yellow armchairs of the media room. They keep company with a Roy Lichtenstein painting and another custom rug—this one featuring a more abstracted image of waves—as well as two Poillerat tables with an impeccable provenance, formerly from the Hamel collection. And in the master bedroom, which features yet another Lichtenstein, there are two French bérgères, circa 1925-30. "These are art pieces," says Bradfield, of the rare period Deco furnishings. "Their shapes and refined presence have allowed me to introduce them as sculpture."

Even the decorative hardware gets its own sculptural twist. Bradfield and associate Roric Tobin worked tirelessly with the jewelry designer John Landrum Bryant on aquatic-themed drawer pulls for the dining room buffet, door handles for the guest room, and faucets and spouts for the powder room (the latter sporting an array of starfish and sea urchins).

RIGHT: Another Lichtenstein painting, this one of water lilies on mylar, hangs in the master suite.

The powder room is a mesmerizing piece of installation art. The owners are avid collectors of paintings by Marc Chagall. Bradfield had the playful idea of reproducing one of the artist's best-known masterpieces, "La Baie des Anges" from 1962, in tiny mosaic tiles. Hand-assembled in Italy and backed with mesh, the larger-than-life image now depicts its mermaid subject soaring amid swirling clouds across three walls of the powder room (the fourth is mirrored and reflects the whole glorious scene). Bradfield also took elements from the painting and had them inset into stone on the floor.

The apartment evokes the life Bradfield is fond of sharing during summers aboard stylish boats in the Mediterranean…like the most legendary of these, the Christina, the 325-foot yacht owned by Aristotle Onassis. The Christina was outfitted with artworks by Renoir, Le Corbusier and de Chirico. Yet Bradfield remembers that its furnishings fell far short of the stupendous caliber of art on the stateroom walls.

That is a trap that the designer, of course, is never at risk of falling into. Bradfield is no stranger to designing yachts, having successfully completed several for clients over the years. And, if this apartment were given leave to set sail, it would surely be the chicest vessel on the high seas.

RIGHT: Bradfield exaggerated the nosegay pattern from the hand-embroidered bed throw, incorporating it into the custom rug. The custom headboard is recessed and flush with the wall surface in the tradition of Jean-Michel Frank.

*" The artist is the hand that sets the
soul vibrating..."*

—Wassily Kandinsky

The history of the Russian *dacha* is steeped in romanticism. The term originally meant "something given," and during the 17th-century reign of Peter the Great, that is precisely what they were: country estates bestowed by the Tsar upon loyal vassals. Later, this architectural form was closely associated with writers (Chekhov's White Dacha in the Crimea, Boris Pasternak's in Peredelkino), many of whom set scenes of their elaborately plotted novels at these familiar country homes (who could forget Dr. Zhivago writing his Lara love poems at Varykino?). Today, the term refers to luxury estates built for the Russian elite near cities and in the posh waterfront communities of Odessa.

OPENING PAGES: The open pattern of the Gilbert Poillerat-inspired front door with gilded scallop shells (left) allows free passage of light and a visual invitation to the Caribbean beyond. An aerial view (right) of Mauricio Lenari's multi-building compound. The colonnaded façade stretches beyond the full length of a New York City block.

BELOW: The arch of the front entry echoes the archway beyond that leads to deep verandas with spellbinding ocean vistas.

RIGHT: Canopied chaises overlook the serene infinity-edge pool.

This home, which its Russian-speaking owners call La Dacha, adds a spectacular new chapter to that history, one that re-imagines the idea of the form for a contemporary international culture. It is, first of all, located far, far afield of the couple's main residence, an expansive Hudson River estate that Bradfield also designed (see *A Hudson River Estate*, page 168). That location would be Terres Basses, an ultra-exclusive enclave on the Caribbean island of St. Martin that is anchored by the renowned La Samanna Hotel (which has attracted everyone from Jacqueline Kennedy Onassis and Richard Nixon to Oprah Winfrey and the designers Dolce and Gabbana). This *dacha* for the 21st century, attests to the power of modern transportation and considerable wealth to render the world a smaller place. Rather than traveling by horse-drawn carriage to the forests outside St. Petersburg, this family flies to their beloved tropical *dacha* by plane.

Instead of being surrounded by woods and cultivated fields like Varykino, La Dacha gazes out over liquid vistas of the Caribbean Sea and the island of Anguilla. In this context, says Bradfield, "The choice of aqua and turquoise was obvious. Otherwise, nothing about it is expected. Like their main home, the influence is very French 1940s, but with a completely different feel."

Originally built by Mauricio Lenari, the multi-building compound was completely renovated by Bradfield to convey "pure escapism," says the designer. "It is open and spacious and embraced by the sun." Like many examples of this vernacular, it serves as a relaxed, kick-your-shoes-off retreat for this couple, their two lovely and adored young daughters, the wife's forever fastidiously groomed mother and a large coterie of friends and relatives. Barbeques and lazy days in the sun are clearly the norm here. Unlike the rustic look of many *dachas*, however, this one is cleanly modern and anchored by classical references.

In the main building, four simple unfluted Doric columns stand at the center of two perpendicular axes, each representing an elegant enfilade. One moves through a custom Art Moderne-style wrought iron front door through the entry hall to the living room, under a wide segmented arch and onto the veranda with the sea beyond; the other proceeds gracefully from the living room, to the hall, into the game room and another outdoor seating area. The four columns support a low ceiling, on either side of which tray ceilings in the living and game rooms soar to 18 feet.

The area delineated by the four columns is the nexus of the main structure from which a sense of casual, understated luxury radiates. Within the home's sprawling open plan, the living room and the game room are cleverly demarcated by identical area rugs executed in complementary, yet contrasting color schemes. The living room version has an ivory ground boasting a loomed turquoise and aqua pattern; the other, an aqua ground with the pattern repeated in turquoise and ivory. An ivory shagreen coffee table with nailhead trim in the living room shares a natural rapport with custom freestanding cabinets of the same materials in the game room. The sharp répartée continues between the game room's parchment lacquer shelving (housing blanc de chine vessels and figurines) and a pair of turquoise lacquer tables in the living room, servicing two corner seating areas. Even the paintings in these rooms, both by Hunt Slonem, converse with and complement each other: in the living room a colorful rabble of butterflies compares to an even denser company of parrots. "If ever there were an appropriate home for these paintings, it is here," says Bradfield contentedly.

LEFT: The central hall leading out to the verandas bisects the great room into a living room (foreground) and a game room with the Moroccan *bhou* beyond.

On the same axis beyond these two spaces, Bradfield called upon his talents as an exotic fantasist. "My client wanted an outdoor Moroccan room," explains the designer. An indigenous gommier tree stood in the space that would eventually become this *bhou* (the Moroccan term for outdoor seating areas). "The architect, Lenari, and I took great lengths to save it," explains Bradfield. The solution called for another tray ceiling over the *bhou* that was semi-detached from the surrounding colonnade. The tree serves as sculpture, and now grows freely in the space between the *bhou* and the colonnade. Because of its exposure to the elements, the de rigueur Moroccan carpet was an impossibility, so Bradfield designed a mosaic floor patterned like a Berber rug instead. "I wanted the room to appear tented," he adds, "but in a modern expression." So the architecture itself became the tenting: alternating Venetian plaster and concrete stripes now descend from the apex of the ceiling, down walls and around six horseshoe arches backed in mirror. The structure encloses low, graphically striped divans that recall harem-style seating.

PREVIOUS PAGES: Hunt Slonem's painting of parrots in the game room, which doubles as a study (left) faces another Slonem painting of butterflies in the living room. The materials—lacquer, shagreen and reversed-tone rugs—unify the spaces.

BELOW: The covered outdoor sitting area is a Moorish flight of fantasy, with horseshoe arches paneled in mirror and a Moroccan-style carpet design executed in mosaic tile.

RIGHT: Bradfield went to great lengths to build the room around a gommier tree. The chair and ottoman are his designs.

Bradfield contrasted the intricate ornament of this *bhou* with a restrained open-air dining room, the walls of which are completely unadorned. "What makes it appear not entirely utilitarian," he says, "is the richness of the tabletop and the glory of Mother Nature." The tabletop showcases a leafy intarsia design, accomplished in lapis lazuli and rare marbles. The form of the custom railings that ring the space, the whole structure cantilevered dramatically over a cliff, echoes the gentle rhythm of ocean waves.

PREVIOUS PAGES: The pool is surrounded by white Triconfort chaises accented by throw pillows covered in an extraordinary blaze of cattleya orchids in a variety of colors.

BELOW: Mother Nature—with her vibrant sunsets and expanse of ocean—is the only art in a dining room that is cantilevered over a cliff.

RIGHT: Blanc de chine singerie hold bouquets of tropical flora, decorating a pietra dura table featuring various marbles and an inlaid lapis border.

"La Dacha is pure escapism. It is open and spacious and embraced by the sun."

—*Geoffrey Bradfield*

In a departure from the Art Moderne styling of many of the spaces, a guest suite references another island culture, that of Cuban sugar plantations. Tobacco-brown lacquered fretwork panels separate the sleeping and sitting room areas, the former displaying a mix of fabrics recalling a hilly Caribbean village; the latter a refined ombré brocade of tropical foliage. One could imagine Ernest Hemingway or Ian Flemming lounging here with paper and pen in hand, composing another rousing novelistic portrait of Caribbean life.

Isolating this residence from the culture of its owners would make it just another (albeit magnificent) Caribbean villa. But, when considered within the context of the clients' background, it truly is a *dacha* for a new age, one that personifies "something given," for it proffers a highly regionalized and contemporary twist on the vernacular. It is tantalizing to imagine what Pasternak would have written in these internationalized times, and whether this modern interpretation of Varykino could have played a more expanded role amid a broader, worldwide literary epic of imperial splendor, revolution, illicit passions and familial love.

PREVIOUS PAGES: A Cuban-themed guest suite has tobacco-lacquered grillwork separating the sitting area from the spacious platform bedroom.

LEFT: A wall of mirrors in the gym and folding glazed doors allow the interior the full embrace of nature. One is surrounded by virtual tropical Eden.

ABOVE: The architecture of the gym, a detached surreal building carved into the volcanic rock.

"*To be an artist is to believe in life.*"

—*Henry Moore*

Diarist and socialite Sir Henry "Chips" Channon described the 2nd Duke of Westminster, Hugh Richard Arthur Grosvenor, as "a mixture of Henry VIII and Lorenzo Il Magnifico, he lived for pleasure—and women." When Bend'Or, as the duke was familiarly known, died, he was the richest man in England, and the £19 million in death duties necessitated the creation of a new sub-department of the Inland Revenue to deal with them. Though later in life "he loathed that grand-scale entertaining," said his fourth wife, Nancy Sullivan, "if you had Grosvenor House, the grandest house in London, it was expected of you."

Clearly, certain addresses demand a certain lifestyle—perhaps no other, nowadays, more than Eaton Square, which Bend'Or developed into one of the city's most coveted enclaves. Its residents have included Neville Chamberlain and Lord Halifax, actors such as Vivien Leigh, Sean Connery and Roger Moore, the philanthropist George Soros and Charles Saatchi and Nigella Lawson. Enter into this exceedingly select club the Iranian-born, British-educated beauty who owns this residence. No stranger to grand-style entertaining, she required a home that was nothing short of ambassadorial in its intent.

To be sure, it is the product of a delicate architectural diplomacy, having arisen from a kind of cross-territorial annexation. What appears to be a single seamless apartment today is, actually, the lateral conversion of two floors of adjacent terrace houses. "It was an Herculean task combining them," recalls Bradfield. "We had to cope with weight-bearing beams that divided the two houses, and with the placement of the chimney breasts, which obstructed a graceful flow of sight and movement between the drawing rooms. So brick by brick, we moved the flues to center the passage. The British masons thought we were insane."

OPENING PAGES: The grandly proportioned foyer features important works by (from foreground to rear) John Chamberlain, François-Xavier Lalanne and Julian Schnabel. The custom railing exhibits subtle Persian ornament.

PREVIOUS PAGES: A pale green reception room precedes a pastel blue drawing room. At left is "White Sky Yellow," an atmospheric abstraction by Julie Hedrick. Below it is a small Christopher Le Brun bronze called "Fortune." A Robert Mangold triangular canvas is to the left of the entrance to the next room; Sheila Mitchell's bronze "Conversation Piece" is to the right.

LEFT: The green reception room, as seen from the blue drawing room, with its custom roundabout and Chagall's "Vase des Fleurs et Femme a L'eventeil." Bradfield had the chimney flues moved to achieve a clear, open symmetry between these spaces that would be visible through a single generous aperture.

The interior scheme also represented a finesse of design détente, as it had to coalesce Eastern and Western aesthetics, as well as ambitious gestures culled from some of Bradfield's favorite historical rooms. "I know how my life works," says the client. "It's a mosaic of many languages, places, cultures and experiences. Geoffrey appreciated that complexity, and we worked hand-in-hand to express it."

The cultural confluence is immediately apparent in the foyer. Wrought iron doors designed "in the vernacular" of Bradfield's constant touchstone, Gilbert Poillerat, open onto a marble-floored entry hall boasting sublime examples of art from two continents: a Lalanne bronze bird, an exuberant John Chamberlain and a painting by Julian Schnabel. A stairway curves gracefully upward along a banister that has been forged with subtle Persian-style ornament.

To the left is a library, and to the right a stately sequence of reception rooms that invite the eye through an ethereal progression of color. It commences with a pale celadon reception room anchored by a trefoil roundabout and surrounded by more stunning art, including paintings by Marc Chagall, Robert Mangold and Julie Hedrick with bronzes by Christopher LeBrun and Sheila Mitchell. The view from here is into the drawing room, this, in pastel blue and also showcasing a cross-cultural mix of furnishings and art. Bradfield researched Persian decoration tirelessly, and it informs the design of two custom carpets—one's pattern a larger abstraction of the other. He blended them with English 18th-century mirrors, a Roman torso circa 100 AD, an Art Moderne coffee table and Rachel Hovnanian's contemporary encaustic painting "Narcissus."

RIGHT: Two custom rugs showcase Persian motifs, one an abstraction of the other, subtly referencing the client's heritage. Rachel Hovnanian's "Narcissus" hangs over the fireplace, flanked by two English 18th-century gilded mirrors from Sotheby's.

The epic renovation took four years, but the absolute rawness of the subsequent space afforded Bradfield the opportunity to indulge flights of fancy drawn from his vast trove of memorable moments in interior design. "I understood that all the material of a literary work was in my past life…," Proust wrote, "stored up by me without my divining its destination or even its survival, as the seed has, in reserve, all the ingredients which will nourish the plant." Proust may have had his Madeleine, but Bradfield has a mind full of ineffaceable rooms to feed his fervid imagination.

One of those served as the catalyst for the dining room, the final chamber in the line of public spaces proceeding from the entry. It was the long-gone dining room of "Chips" Channon and his wife, the former Lady Honor Guinness, which had been located nearby on Belgrave Square. Decorated in the 1930s by Stephane Boudin, Channon wanted this Bavarian Rococo fantasy to rival Amalienburg, the famous hunting lodge on the grounds of the Nymphenburg Palace in Munich. "I think it is going to be stupendous," wrote Channon rather immodestly. "There is to be a small anteroom opening into a gallery— orange and silver like the Amalienburg; then another door, and then I hope, stupefaction… It will shimmer in blue and silver, and have an ochre and silver gallery leading to it. It will shock, and perhaps stagger London."

Bradfield's interpretation certainly stupefies and staggers, but without resorting to the ostentation of Channon's dining room (or his prose). It adopts the color scheme and the mirrored walls, but translates them into a modern idiom by reducing the excessive ornament. "It's a pocket of pure rhapsody and make-believe," admits Bradfield with obvious delight. He infused this room, too, with the Eastern sensibility of its owner in the form of a lapis and ivory mosaic border on the marble floor, as well as framed panels of chinoiserie floating on the mirrored walls.

RIGHT: Inspired by "Chips" Channon's 1940s silver-and-blue dining room, this one reduces ornament and injects Eastern references such as framed chinoiserie panels and a blue-and-silver mirror mosaic border inlaid into the crema marfil floor.

FOLLOWING PAGES: Frank Auerbach's "Head of JYM," from the Marlborough Gallery London, hangs over the library mantelpiece and is an exciting contrast against the blue mohair wall covering. The custom rug was inspired by Japanese woodcuts. Rich walnut paneling and bookcases house an exceptional collection of bound first editions.

The color scheme in the master bedroom—ivory and charcoal gray—had its germination years before, when Bradfield traveled to Mexico City to decorate a home that had formerly belonged to legendary beauty Merle Oberon and the industrialist Bruno Pagliai. "Her dressing room blew me away," he recalls. "It was dark, charcoal gray and mirrors. These moments remain with one." But, for this dressing room, Bradfield and his client drew upon yet another favorite space: the colonnade of arched doors in the grand hall at Claridge's. As philosopher Gaston Bachelard observed, "the surest sign of wonder is exaggeration." In this sumptuous room, a princess is completely surrounded by mirrors set behind wrought iron swags and tassels that have been finished in white gold.

The master bedroom itself trades on Bradfield's love of 1940s films. It was inspired, he says, by the blonde bombshell Jean Harlow. Yet, the room enters irreversibly into the 21st century with the introduction of a black patinated bronze Jacques Lipchitz sculpture and, even more appropriately for the cavalcade of historical references, a pair of Hunt Slonem butterfly paintings. The latter recalls the engravings of famous botanists and entomologists, like Gustav Mann and Obadiah Westwood, that were all the rage in 18th- and 19th-century English homes.

Despite the specific inspirations Bradfield is tapping, however, there is nothing derivative or predictable about the way it all comes together. To quote Proust again, "A work of art that contains theories is like an object on which the price tag has been left." Bradfield never trucks in the obvious.

"The ingredients of my designs are fairly principled," says the designer. "But, it's a boon when a client has a cogent point of view. It's that shot of paprika, and it ups the ante." Certainly the stakes were very high in this gamble. However, with the finesse required of all foreign affairs, the multilateral negotiation of personal inspirations, opinions, predilections and other disparate factors achieves complete entente.

PREVIOUS PAGES: The master bedroom has a dramatic vaulted ceiling and, above the side tables, Hunt Slonem paintings of butterflies that recall botanical renderings, familiar in 19th-century English interiors. A Jacques Lipchitz sculpture is in the foreground.

RIGHT: The dressing room in the master suite was patterned after the grand hall of Claridge's Hotel. The wrought iron swags and tassels on the mirrors are finished in white gold.

"*I try to apply colors like words that shape poems, like notes that shape music.*"

—Joan Miró

In 1947, Christian Dior sent his ultra-luxurious "New Look" down the Paris runways. Costumes with smartly tailored tops broke out at the wasp waists of his young models in sharply accentuated flared skirts. The silhouette was totally unexpected, and it signaled a renewed worldly optimism. It was an instant international sensation.

Balance was the key, in Dior's case, between precision and exuberance. And, this idea of balance is exactly what Bradfield summoned for a luxury high-rise apartment overlooking Lake Powai in one of the most exclusive enclaves of Mumbai. The results juggle much more than just precision and exuberance, and they are just as unexpected as the fashion designer's "New Look," especially in a land often given to shows of Mughal splendor.

OPENING PAGES: Bradfield designed the staff's saffron livery in shantung silk.

BELOW LEFT: The living room, with its view of Lake Powai. The sisal is handpainted with an Art Moderne pattern.

BELOW RIGHT: Paintings by Barbara Rae depicting landscapes of the Karoo in South Africa...visible over a luxurious custom tufted ottoman.

BOTTOM RIGHT: The Baskerville painting "Sultan on Horseback," along with the persimmon accents, provide a Mughal feel for the otherwise contemporary décor.

RAJASTHAN

THE UNFORGETTABLE
MAHARAJAS

Lustre Press
Roli Books

INDIA

The clients—with whom Bradfield had very successful collaborations on a Notting Hill townhouse and would later assist with the renovation of their 10th-century Tuscan farmhouse—had been relocated to India for two years by the husband's employer, an international banking colossus. The floor plan, a blandly rectilinear arrangement of rooms, reflected the more controlled half of Bradfield's own 'New Look'-style approach. An executive of this stature is obliged to employ a large staff, so he and his wife required an area where they could find privacy and solitude. Bradfield responded by carving out a separate suite from the larger floor plan that accommodated an entrance, master bedroom, dressing rooms, two master baths and a study—in short, a lavish cocoon for their well-being.

The couple owned some beautiful contemporary art, much of it South African, which weighed in on the more exuberant end of the scale. The paintings' pungent colors—sunset oranges, flame reds, saffron yellows and lime greens—happily comprised a palette already ubiquitous in the Indian subcontinent, so they were a serendipitous springboard for Bradfield's design scheme.

PREVIOUS PAGES: Paintings by Julie Hedrick are framed by two of four tree branch floor lamps by Marsia Holzer that bracket the living room.

LEFT: A glass-topped Poillerat-inspired table and a skeletal console by Diego Giacometti add visual interest to the dining area without obstructing the view.

ABOVE: The studio of Julie Hedrick in Kingston, New York.

"It is typical of Geoffrey to instinctively make choices around art that resonate with his clients' preferences and stories," says the owner. Speaking specifically about two abstract landscapes over the living room sofa, she adds, "These pictures, which were in our collection, are in fact painted by one of Scotland's most sought-after contemporary colorists, Barbara Rae, but represent one of South Africa's most beautiful landscapes in the Karoo. Placing them in our Mumbai apartment was inspirational."

Another designer might have deployed these hues with a heavier hand, in yard upon yard of silk upholstery or drapery, for example, tilting toward a more cliché Eastern opulence. Respecting the modern frame of the penthouse, however, Bradfield, applied his typical restraint, choosing textured ecru walls to showcase the paintings, along with discreet dashes of persimmon. Additionally, Bradfield drew color from Lake Powai and its surrounding flora in the form of sumptuous tufted and fringed jade green ottomans. And, he adds, "I had 16 full-height doors lacquered in jade green to maximize drama."

THESE PAGES: A fine example of the artist William Kentridge (above) completes the north wall of a guest bedroom. Crystal and bronze Gilbert Poillerat sconces (right) flank the headboard in the master bedroom.

Furnishings struck a similar equilibrium. Bradfield incorporated humble Indian materials such as sisal and wicker, but elevated them through a more refined approach: the wicker itself boasts comfortably contemporary silhouettes rather than Victorian Raj-issue ornament, and the sisal rug was handpainted in a scrolling 1940s classical design. Two pairs of iron floor lamps anchoring the living room have modern branch-like forms that complement the clients' more rustically forged Diego Giacometti tables. And, Eastern curve-edged tables à la Jean-Michel Frank offer voluptuous Deco counterpoints to the sober square-armed contemporary sofas in the living room. The mix is international, referencing local culture as well as that of Europe and America.

Everywhere Bradfield has balanced control with flourish, the contemporary with the classical, smoothness with texture, Oriental with Occidental. It's the last sort of interior one would expect to see in Mumbai…unless, perhaps, one were Christian Dior himself.

" *All I can do will only ever be a faint image of what I see.* "

—*Alberto Giacometti*

History can sometimes feel like an albatross, particularly in the field of hospitality design. Absolute authenticity in royal palaces and museum environments is one thing. But, at the historic inns we retreat to for rest and relaxation, we crave modern conveniences and do not want to live in the frugal manner of the Founding Fathers. A little of that vintage charm tends to go a very long way.

So, when Bradfield received the commission to renovate and redesign the interiors of the Equinox Resort in Manchester, Vermont—one of the oldest continually operating resorts in the country—it came freighted with a slavish historicity and ample opportunity to become ensnared in nostalgia and sentimentality. On the National Register of Historic Places, it began life more than 240 years ago as the Marsh Tavern in 1769. Since then, it has hosted revolutionary gatherings (Ethan Allen's brother, Ira, proposed seizing Tory properties here to equip an anti-colonialist regiment) and presidents (Ulysses S. Grant, Benjamin Harrison, Teddy Roosevelt and William Howard Taft). Mary Todd Lincoln so loved the place that eventually her daughter and son-in-law, Mary Lincoln and Charles Isham, bought the establishment in 1905, and Mary's brother Robert built his Georgian Revival estate, Hildene, nearby.

That is a lot of tradition to shoulder. But, Bradfield approached the project with Alberto Giacometti's admonition in mind: "…the object of art is not to reproduce reality, but to create a reality of the same intensity." The $20 million restoration introduces modern luxury to a 200-room resort that, while charming in its way, had become quaint and sadly dated. "They approached me because they did not want to create period rooms," explains Bradfield. "They were emphatic, in that they wanted a contemporary point of view that would also capture the dignity of its history."

THESE PAGES: The hotel in a typical New England autumn setting (top left) and the resort's façade (bottom left). Seating arrangements off the great room. Bradfield, with the support of the architect, had the fireplace moved from a corner to be centered on the feature wall.

The first order of business was to reconfigure the layouts of the public spaces. A guest suite sandwiched between the restaurant and lobby, for example, had always been plagued by the noise and traffic of guests coming to and fro. Bradfield proposed converting the space into The Falcon Bar, which today is a handsome mahogany-paneled lounge with art that references the raptor expeditions the resort conducts through the local British School of Falconry. Bradfield also suggested enlarging the verandas and terraces, extending them along the rear of the main building to create connected outdoor access to many of the public spaces. In addition, this extension allowed the designer to introduce a giant fire pit that has become a popular gathering place for the guests as well as for residents of the hamlet.

Inexplicably, the window treatments in the great room, which was situated at the very end of the corridor leading from the entrance, actually obscured scenic views of Mt. Equinox, at over 3,800 feet the most spectacular peak of the Taconic Range. The dim and uninviting space had become little more than a way station for guests en route to other activities. "The room looked unloved, as if it had been abandoned by its suitor, not unlike Miss Haversham's wedding banquet in *Great Expectations*," recalls Bradfield.

The designer, with his associate Roric Tobin, lightened the palette and created simpler, cleaner window treatments that completely transformed the room. "Now people sit there and have coffee or read the paper, look out at the mountains and onto the terrace," says Tobin.

The great room décor exemplifies the sort of perfectly calibrated balance between history and contemporary panache that Bradfield's clients were seeking. Instead of the de rigueur colonial-era wing chairs and 18th-century English furniture, the designer imbued the room with a sense of history that mined a more recent decorative vein, one that defined our idea of modern luxury in the 1930s and '40s—Art Deco. Comfortable chairs upholstered in forest green pony hide are reinterpreted French Deco designs that mix with more classical elements like fringed banquettes and an outsized roundabout. Bradfield also drew upon the metalwork of Diego Giacometti for his custom lighting, side tables and consoles. Giacometti's bronze incarnations of flora and fauna were ideally suited to the sylvan setting of the Equinox, but, they also added artistic weight that elevated the great room and adjacent lobby spaces above the usual standardized commercial interiors.

"My late partner Jay Spectre and I visited Giacometti's studio in Paris frequently during the last years of his life," remembers Bradfield. "We would always take him a flagon of Kentucky bourbon and invariably have lunch at Café Barola, the restaurant across the way. He was such a great man, a veritable giant in the art world of his age. These furnishings are an homage to him. I took no liberties; they are all authentic reproductions." The rug in this room also references the sculptor's zoomorphic imagery. Bradfield's inventively organic design for the floor covering, beyond the main reception, was deliberately freeform to make it easily adaptable to differently proportioned rooms, hallways and landings.

Baskervill Architects successfully expedited the production of Bradfield's designs, translating them into durable contract-grade furnishings. "We explained to them, that there were certain things, like the lighting, on which we felt they could not compromise," recalls Tobin. And indeed, the patinated bronze sconces and pendant lamps are expertly wrought and look as if they were produced in Giacometti's own studio.

OPENING AND THESE PAGES: The great room had been dark and obscured views of the mountain. Bradfield and Tobin lightened the palette and made it more inviting and hospitable.

PREVIOUS PAGES: A detail of a Giacometti-inspired console (left) and the sitting room, with its luxe furnishings, fireplace and photographic vintage views of the historic hotel.

"I visited Diego Giacometti's studio in Paris frequently during the last years of his life…these furnishings are an homage to him."

—*Geoffrey Bradfield*

ABOVE: The west façade of the hotel and its great lawn.

RIGHT: Connecting the public spaces with a deep terrace allowed the designer to introduce seating and a fire pit, now a popular gathering place for guests, as well as residents of the hamlet.

"The owners were very emphatic that they wanted a contemporary point of view that would also capture the dignity of the resort's history."

—Geoffrey Bradfield

"Vintage subject matter, captured in black and white photography, references the resort's celebrated past."

—Geoffrey Bradfield

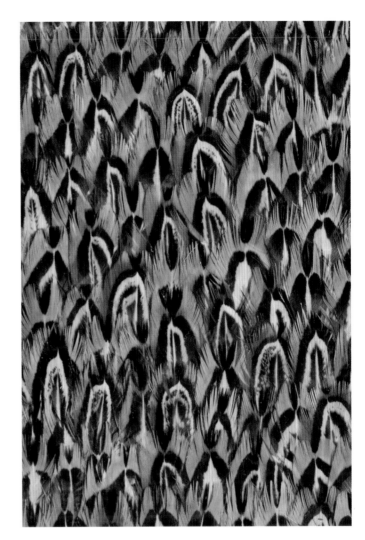

ABOVE: The mahogany-paneled claret-and-cream-colored bar displays falcon-themed photography as art.

RIGHT: Bradfield suggested filling in the panels of the walls with falcon feathers (top). A live falcon from the school (bottom) is held aloft in front of one of the photographs.

Throughout the other rooms, the team's choices consistently contemporize historical references in subtle ways. Rugs in the library and the Marsh Tavern, for instance, are newer, brighter takes on Tartan plaid, their large-format patterning and lighter palette placing them squarely in the 21st century. And, enlarged black-and-white photography, a distinctly modern art form, accomplishes a similar function; the vintage subject matter references the resort's celebrated past.

LEFT: The Marsh Tavern's traditional wing-and-Windsor-chair surroundings get a graphic modern makeover with a boldly oversize plaid patterned rug.

ABOVE: The Chop House is located in the oldest part of the building and boasts a fireplace with an 1832 quoin added by the Orvis family.

FOLLOWING PAGES: The firelit library marries contemporary comfort and a traditional color scheme. The rug is another variation on Tartan plaid.

LEFT: Bradfield designed the carpeting throughout, using free-form patterns that could be adapted to hallways of different widths.

BELOW: The duplex Eisenhower Suite, with a steeple view, showcases a blue, beige and brown palette—one of several color schemes introduced by the designer.

RIGHT: In all the guest rooms, Bradfield deployed blown-up vintage photographs of the property (top) in lieu of paintings or the de rigueur insipid hotel "art." A skillful blending of patterns highlights the view of the gold domed courthouse beyond the window.

For bedrooms and suites, the management team selected a blue, beige and brown palette amongst the various color choices Bradfield proposed. "The presentation," recalls Bradfield, "was very elaborate, with models and floor plans and a variety of color combinations." To this scheme he added dark wood furnishings, deepening the sense of richness. But, he kept the look modern not only in the forms of the furnishings, but by dressing the case goods with a quintessentially modern material: brushed stainless steel.

"If you own a landmark hotel, you want something that is unique," concludes Bradfield. The designer's reinvention of this 17-building complex certainly accomplishes that one-of-a-kind exclusivity. In fact, it is so successful that the Equinox Resort is one of the latest pearls to have been added to the string of establishments known as The Starwood Luxury Collection, a glittering ensemble of over 60 of the world's finest hotels and resorts sprinkled throughout 26 countries. It is also responsible for luring Land Rover to Manchester, where the company now conducts 4x4 off-road driving expeditions for Equinox guests on the more than 1,300 acres of woodland that surround the hotel. Fitting accolades that deservedly dovetail with one of the most historically prestigious guest lists of any establishment in America, one that is sure to attract more presidents and other highly notable callers in the years to come.

"My evil genius Procrastination has whispered me to tarry 'til a more convenient season," said Mary Todd Lincoln. Bradfield has given her spirit a place in which she would enjoy tarrying in our present age.

"The space within becomes the reality
of the building."

—Frank Lloyd Wright

As architects and designers know all too well, building anything in New York is a complex proposition that involves layer upon layer of bureaucracy. It is a minor miracle, then, that the Icon Group, developers of 985 Park Avenue, were able not only to build the first new condominium along this august promenade in decades, but that the result so seamlessly blends in with its surroundings while retaining its own integrity.

Costas Kondylis, whose accepted style has made him the preferred architect of Donald Trump, departed from his norm to design a contextual structure that infuses the classical pre-war aesthetic of Emery Roth and Rosario Candela with more glass and less ornament. For the interiors, Icon's partners—Todd Cohen, Terrence Lowenberg and Michael Miller— sought someone whose sense of style could also bridge Beaux-Arts and modernist idioms, and they found a natural partner in Geoffrey Bradfield. "From the lobby to the penthouse," says the website for the building, "every inch of 985 Park is a tribute to Mr. Bradfield's imagination."

PREVIOUS PAGES: The slim façade of modernity (left) amid Park Avenue's stately pre-war dignity. The lobby (right) mixes classical and Art Moderne elements with a sophisticated, contemporary gray palette.

BELOW: The entrance beckons with nickel-plated doors set into the unadorned modern façade.

RIGHT: The mirror-lined entry corridor with its luxurious polished marble floors and Bradfield's original rendering of the room.

985

That imagination purveys a platinum glamour that perfectly suited the 15-story building, which comprises just seven apartments—five duplexes and two triplexes. "Period styles come and go, and sometimes come again," says Bradfield. "I am an ardent modernist, yet I look to the past for inspiration, drawing on classical revival to create interiors both rich in history and alive with 21st-century sophistication."

Once inside the elegant glass and nickel-plated doors (the design recalls the French Art Moderne movement), visitors are introduced to a marble-floor lobby lined with a graceful procession of pilasters and boasting a richly coffered ceiling overhead. Walls and furniture are pale gray, creating an instant air of tailored elegance. Custom chairs with nickel-plated feet and scrolled arms, as well as a desk of French Rococo form stripped of its usual ormolu flourishes, balance the orthogonal order of the reception area.

The apartments themselves offer a plenitude of light care of floor-to-ceiling windows, light that is repeated and amplified by mirrored facing walls. Classical references—pilasters, mantelpieces and moldings—impart a substantial foundation to what is essentially a modern living room. Herringbone-patterned wood floors add natural warmth.

BELOW: Bradfield's concept for the decoration of one of the living rooms.

RIGHT: The living room has classical elements and a modern, mullioned, floor-to-ceiling glass wall, allowing beautiful views of the avenue and Central Park beyond.

The bathrooms and kitchens are more rigorously contemporary while sparing not one iota of luxury. The materials are classic staples of high-end construction—Thassos marble and Kashmir white onyx, for instance—but, they are deployed with a view to younger modern tastes. Bradfield brings the clean lines of Italian cabinetry to the kitchen and a rectilinear double vanity of rich dark wood in the master bath. These choices of stark contrasts give the spaces a more adventurous edge than one is used to seeing along the old-monied, conservative interiors of the Park Avenue corridor.

On the strength of Bradfield's design for the temporary 72nd Street sales office—a lavishly appointed prototype of the living room in one of the apartments—sales moved briskly. Without a word of advertising, the developers immediately had 200 prospective buyers on their waiting list. "We hit the ground running and sold two apartments in the first six weeks despite the traditional summer slowdown," says Reba Miller, principal of the firm handling the marketing for the building. Six months thereafter, all the multimillion-dollar units (with average prices of $2,300 per square foot) had been purchased.

"What these two young men in their 20s accomplished was an absolute coup and truly phenomenal," says Bradfield admiringly. True. But, it is also a testament to Bradfield's love of "functional opulence." His design for 985 Park, he says, "is a composition of both Old World refinement and stylish contemporary vigor." It's a composition that disarmed the traditionalist naysayers and skeptics who doubted Park Avenue would ever see a new, much less modern, façade, one that has brought this billionaire row's legendary fame into an entirely new generation.

"I am definitely hoping to be in touch with my subconscious. I expect a call any minute…"

—Julian Schnabel

In 1950, the innovative architectural firm Skidmore Owings & Merrill erected the iconic Manhattan House. "It typifies New York in one of its most confident eras," observes Bradfield, "a period of American design coming of age on the world stage. There is absolutely no reference to European sensibilities." So, when designing an interior scheme for a living room in that landmark building during the 2008 Kips Bay Show House, Bradfield blazed a provocative path. "The living room of this apartment captures the original spirit of these pioneers," avers the designer.

As imagined by Bradfield, "It is home to an art dealer and, as such, is also a foil to his ever-changing art collection. The interior takes on the feel of an impromptu gallery." This gallery owner, one supposes, is visibly youthful and hip, with modern attitudes that naturally draw him to Pop Art, the groundbreaking movement sparked in the 1950s that brazenly challenged the elitist notion that popular culture had no place in the rarefied world of fine art.

Like a young man beginning to trust his own tastes and assert his own opinions, this punked environment struts with a fresh self-assurance. Unafraid of color, the living room walls announce their presence with vertical surfaces bathed in bold burnt orange lacquer. With their saturated depth of color, they are a perfect counterpoint to the graphic flatness of three huge paintings by the artist duo Manolo Caceres and José Miranda.

OPENING PAGES: Burnt orange lacquer walls set the dramatic scene for contemporary art and a mix of custom and 1950s furniture. The paintings are by Spanish artist team Caceres+Miranda.

ABOVE: In the consummately art-directed world of this studio, a wall dedicated to auction catalogues becomes its own minimalist sculpture.

RIGHT: The dining area features gothic-shaped Fairbanks chairs on acrylic legs and a 1960s chrome table. A 1950s light fixture from Salibello looks, in Bradfield's words, "like a smoldering orange sun."

"It is home to an art dealer and, as such, is also a foil to his ever-changing art collection. The interior takes on the feel of an impromptu gallery."

—Geoffrey Bradfield

Bradfield's choice of art is no accident. Caceres+Miranda are famous in their native Spain and around the world for appropriating images of Maoist propaganda—rendering them in flat black and white to appear commercially printed—then placing them against a variety of backgrounds with other art-historical references, in this case, factoryscapes reminiscent of those by American Precisionist painter Charles Sheeler. This body of work is called "Panta Rei" ("everything changes"), and it radiates an outlook that is unremittingly progressive. "We are only interested in the optimism and idealism of people…not the political subterfuge of the leadership," Caceres has said. These are ideals that have seduced young men since the beginning of human existence.

Bradfield perfectly pairs the "Panta Rei" paintings with one of Joel Perlman's gravity-defying scrap metal sculptures, and lights the scene with chrome industrial-looking tripod lamps that carry through the idea of mechanical mass production implicit in the art.

PREVIOUS PAGES: The inventively varied seating gathers around a Karl Springer mother-of-pearl table. Included are a round Bradfield-designed ottoman and a slipper chair with elaborate nailhead trim, from his collection for Stark, and a pair of quintessentially 1950s chairs.

ABOVE: A vintage Macassar ebony desk on the right, across from a Joel Perlman industrial iron sculpture. Caceres+Miranda's paintings interpose Sheeler-like factoryscapes with characters appropriated from Maoist propaganda.

RIGHT: In the window, one of a pair of life-size bronze puma sculptures by Gwen Murrell contemplates the Manhattan skyline.

Yet, a room devoted single-mindedly to Industrial Age idealism could lean perilously close to glibness or, worse, naiveté. Bradfield steers clear, grounding the space with classic mid-century modern furniture. Then, he gives the room a shot of contemporary luxury by combining the vintage furnishings with custom upholstered pieces showcasing the designer's own textiles for Stark. The furniture, for the most part, is skeletal. But, some pieces—a vintage Karl Springer mother-of-pearl coffee table and Bradfield-designed round ottoman and skirted chair—provide enough mass and volume to keep the paintings from completely overwhelming the composition. Also balancing the enormous canvases is a wall of built-in bookcases that house auction catalogues.

"True chic shuns convention," says Bradfield. This room, in which not a single element feels expected, corroborates his ideal. It bespeaks masculine energy and creature comforts and yet fulfills his steadfast commitment to 21st-century style.

"To see far is one thing...
going there is another."

—*Constantin Brancusi*

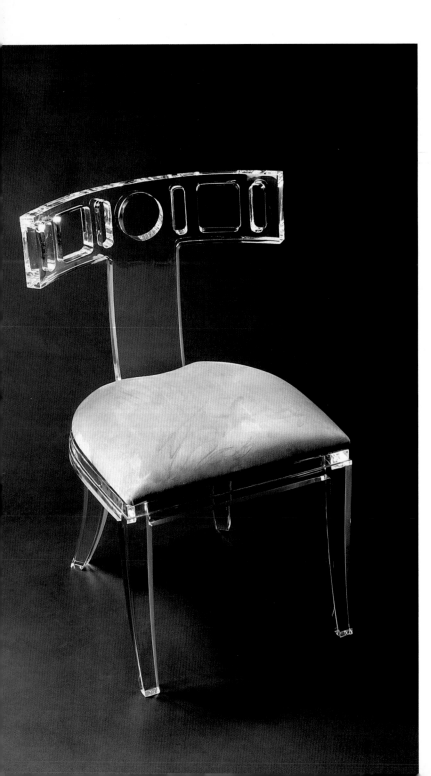

"Any designer who is passionate about what he does and has a strong point of view is mindful of creating a legacy," says Bradfield. "But, when one has been fortunate enough to be recognized for one's work, you like to feel not only that you are leaving a footprint, but also that you are giving back."

The germination of this altruism actually took root in South Africa in the lap of his family home, where the natural generosity of his parents instructed by example. Long before his career set off on its meteoric climb or his clients and social circle expanded to include many great philanthropists, Bradfield shared Ralph Waldo Emerson's simple belief that "The greatest gift is a portion of thyself."

In the 1980s, through his friend David Hanks, the curator of the Stewart Program for modern design at the Stewart Museum in Montreal, he decided to do just that. "He has always been interested in collecting," says Hanks of Bradfield. "And, he was interested in museums and what their objectives could achieve. He began donating early on, even when he had very little money to make such donations."

In the 1980s, Hanks introduced the designer to Craig Miller, then Associate Curator of 20th-Century Architecture and Design at the Metropolitan Museum of Art. "The Met represents a superlative level of academic scholarship," says Bradfield. "It has been an unfailing resource in my life. In this country, considered the New World, we don't enjoy through heritage the great palaces taken for granted in Europe. The Met is more than a museum; it is our equivalent of Versailles. It's our treasure trove of so many civilizations." So, he resolved to demonstrate his gratitude to the institution that had so enriched him over the years.

Miller assessed the Met's holdings and determined that its acquisitions of industrial textiles had been uneven and wanting. With the curator's direction, Bradfield began acquiring this category in earnest and gave the fabrics and objects he amassed to the museum. "Geoffrey helped establish the core of the Met's 20th-century textile collection," says Miller. "The pieces range from the Art Deco period to Memphis and include such major designers as Ruhlmann, the Eameses and du Pasquier."

Bradfield has continued to donate many other furnishings, such as an original Bertoia chair and ottoman. "When the Ruhlmann show was mounted at the Met," points out Hanks, "there were important textiles donated by Geoffrey in the exhibition."

His generosity has not been reserved exclusively for exalted, all-encompassing institutions like the Metropolitan. Hanks also facilitated Bradfield's considerable donations to The Stewart Museum, a private institution dedicated to the acquisition of artifacts, documents and illustrations "that show the presence and influence of European civilization on the history of New France and North America."

Liliane M. Stewart, the widow of museum founder David MacDonald Stewart and the head of the MacDonald Stewart Foundation, feels that in Bradfield, they have gained a patron with a curator's discriminating taste. "Geoffrey Bradfield's extraordinary eye for objects has not only enhanced many of the beautiful interiors he designed throughout the world, but has also benefited our collection in Montreal," she says. "He is our most generous American donor of design objects, helping to make the collection one of the most important of its type in North America. I am delighted that his generosity has included gifts of some of the most rare examples of 20th-century design, such as the chess table, a biomorphic masterpiece by the American sculptor Isamu Noguchi. His donation of significant textiles by renowned designers reflects his special interest in this medium. We salute our dear friend for this spirit of sharing, which will allow these beautiful objects to be enjoyed by so many."

As with the Met, Bradfield continues to give, says Hanks, pointing out collections of silver, ceramics, glass and furniture that have flowed from the designer for years. "He is attached to very little; he never keeps things," says Hanks. "It's part of his ongoing quest for the new. One learns from the objects one collects, and then you're on to something else. Geoffrey's donations parallel with the interiors he does for himself."

Bradfield's legacy is now entering a new and ascendant chapter. For the first time in his career, his furniture designs, particularly his work in acrylic, are being recognized with a solo exhibition at Chelsea's Sebastian+Barquet gallery. Latin American paintings dealer Ramis Barquet, according to the savvy online magazine *Artnet*, has "emerged as a mega-player in design." With locations in New York and London, he has elevated the profiles of legendary designers like George Nakashima, Jean Prouvé and Gio Ponti, as well as contemporary legends-in-the-making such as Marc Newsom and Vladimir Kagan.

"The gallery devotes a show each year to a designer whose work occupies a significant place within the contemporary design landscape," says Sebastian+Barquet creative director Nicholas Kilner, "and in the spring of 2009, dedicated an exhibition to the designs of Geoffrey Bradfield."

Kilner feels Bradfield's work is "an intuitive reflection of eclectic contemporary tastes. Among the greater attributes of the designer's work is his ability to create modern interiors that make subtle visual reference to period forms and styles without appearing nostalgic or outdated; environments that succeed in being entirely 'of the moment,' while simultaneously aware of their heritage."

Kilner also lauds Bradfield for exploring the unique properties of acrylic, a material, he points out, that has been around since the 1930s but reached its heyday in the 1960s and '70s with the work of Charles Hollis Jones. Out of favor in the last 20 years, he credits Bradfield with spearheading the resurrection of acrylic's popularity and, in addition, pushing the boundaries of the material through his own designs.

"Bradfield's work marks a return to an under-explored medium that he handles with commendable skill and sensitivity," says Kilner. "Through considered appropriation and reinterpretation of past forms and styles, Bradfield succeeds in creating something that, in his blending of the past and the present, is fundamentally 'of the moment' and uniquely his own. The coexistence of traditional values and modern aesthetics make for work that is at once familiar and new."

Kilner arrives at Ned Rorem's incandescent conclusion that "In the act of stealing, the artist is so guilty that he tries to cover his tracks. The act of covering his tracks is the act of creation." This compendium of classic modern design consolidates Bradfield's aspiration and brilliantly achieves *ex arte pulchritudo*: "beauty through art."

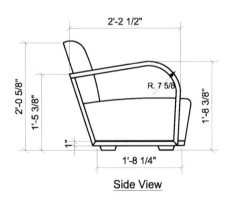

Side View

2'-2 1/2"
2'-0 5/8"
1'-5 3/8"
R. 7 5/8"
1'-8 3/8"
1"
1'-8 1/4"

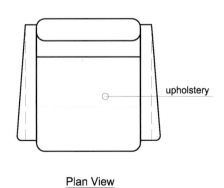

upholstery

Plan View

BELOW: The award-winning "Coco" chair, Bradfield's homage to Gabrielle Chanel—declared the "little black dress" of furniture.

GEOFFREY BRADFIELD FURNITURE COLLECTION · CLUB CHAIR · PLAN, VIEW & ELEVATION

ABOVE: Geoffrey Bradfield and his associate, Company Vice President Roric Tobin (left), are in constant motion. The firm's New York-based office, as well as satellite companies in Palm Beach, the Emirates and Qatar, keep these gentlemen constantly jetting from one continent to the next... catapulting their brand onto the global stage.

"*Although some feeling for beauty is perhaps universal among men, the same cannot be said of the understanding of beauty.*"

—Borromini, *The Principles of Aesthetics*